GOLDEN WARRIORS OF THE UKRAINIAN STEPPES

Catalogue of an exhibition of gold treasures from
the Ukrainian Historic Treasures Museum, National Museum of Ukrainian History

City of Edinburgh Art Centre
14 August - 17 October 1993

City of Edinburgh Museums and Art Galleries, 1993
ISBN No : 0 9050 7251 0

Exhibition Organising Committee, Kiev

Convener : S.M. Chaykovskiy. Zh.G. Arustamyan, Yu.A. Belan, S.A. Berezovaya, B.B. Garbuz, T.G. Degtyareva-Kapnik, L.S. Klochko, S.A. Koretskaya, E.P. Podvysotskaya, E.V. Starchenko, M.S. Strelets, V.M. Khardayev, T.F. Shamina.

Costume reconstructions: L.S. Klochko, A.I. Minzhilin.

Exhibition Organising Committee, Edinburgh

Convener : Herbert Coutts. D. Patterson, A. Topp, J. Warrilow, L. Stothers, D. Janes, S. Marwick, S. Mullen, R. McLean, D. Tait, A. Forsyth

Catalogue

Articles and catalogue entries : S. M. Chaykovskiy, V. M. Khardayev, Yu.A. Belan, S.A. Berezovaya, L.S. Klochko, S.A. Koretskaya, T.F. Shamina, M.S. Strelets, T.G. Degtyareva, Zh.G. Arustamyan, B.B. Garbuz.

Illustrations : P.L. Kornienko (p. 16, 19), M.I. Reyter (p. 12), M.V. Rusyaeva (p. 53, 63), B. Reid(backcover)

Photography : Atelier Kraftner, Vienna
(Cat. nos. 13, 23, 39 : National History Museum of Ukraine)

Translation of Russian text : Caroline Horne, Geoffrey H. Harper

Catalogue Design : City of Edinburgh Museum and Galleries Design Section

Editor : H. Coutts
© Copyright of English edition, City of Edinburgh Museums and Art Galleries, Department of Recreation, City of Edinburgh `District Council 1993

Exhibition Presented By
The City of Edinburgh District Council and the National History Museum of Ukraine

Sponsored by

Assisted by

Contents

Foreword

This exhibition is the fruit of friendship between Edinburgh and its newest twin-city, Kiev the capital of the Ukraine. It brings to the United Kingdom for the first time an array of precious artifacts, which represent the high art of successive waves of peoples who swept over the Pontic steppes during three millenia. A great debt of gratitude is owed to the Ukrainian Government and the Director of the National History Museum of the Ukraine for agreeing to release such important national treasures for display here.

With one exception, the exhibits are drawn from the extensive collections of the Museum of Historical Treasures, a branch of the National History Museum, which is located in the beautiful Kiev - Pechersk monastery complex. Founded in 1051, the monastery developed into one of the great religious and cultural centres of Kiev. It is particularly appropriate that collections reflecting the genius of generation upon generation of Ukrainian master craftsmen should be displayed here. Recently, following the collapse of Communist rule in the Ukraine, monks have returned to part of the site. Once again, the timeless pursuit of the goals of holiness and art are in close communion.

Exhibitions such as this are expensive to organise and would not be possible without the help of sponsors. Generous support has been received from "The Scotsman" newspaper, the Museums and Galleries Commission, the Scottish Office, Nimmos Colour Printers, Austrian Airlines and Ethicon Ltd. Additional assistance has been given by the Edinburgh Tattoo, SMT coach company, the Scottish Tourist Board, Lothian and Borders Police and the Edinburgh Ukrainian Community.

This project has benefited from the enthusiastic support of Councillor Steve Cardownie, Convener of the District Council's Recreation Committee, Mr. Roger Jones, Director of Recreation, and many other Recreation Department and District Council colleagues. Finally, I wish to place on record my sincere thanks to security, technical, design, conservation, curatorial and clerical staff of the City Museums and Art Galleries. It is their commitment, enthusiasm and sheer hard work which have brought this exhibition to fruition.

Herbert Coutts
City Curator

Tripolski Culture	5000 - 3000 BC
Catacomb Grave Culture	2100 - 1700 BC
Corded Ware Culture	1700 - 1500 BC
Timber Grave Culture	1600 - 1200 BC
Sabatinovka Culture	1400 - 1200 BC
Belozerka Culture	1200 - 1000 BC
Cimmerians	10 - 7th c. BC
Scythians	7 - 3rd c. BC
Sarmatians	2nd c. BC - 3rd c. AD
Greek City States	6th c. BC - 3rd c. AD
Huns	4 - 5th c. AD
Avars	6 - 7th c. AD
Slavs	6 - 8th c. AD
Khazars	7th - 8th c. AD
Kiev Rus	9 - 13th c. AD
Pechenegs	10 - 12th c. AD
Polovtsy	11 - 13th c. AD
Mongols (Golden Horde)	13 - 14th c. AD

Modern Ukraine

7

Introduction

"Treasures of the Ukraine" is the name often given to the Museum of Historical Treasures to emphasize the significance of its collections. It is no exaggeration to say that its collections are becoming famous the world over, and this has been made possible by the enormous amount of work which the museum has undertaken in researching the collections and in informing the public about them. Indeed these are priceless treasures, representing the culture not only of our own people but of the whole world.

A start was only made on assembling the museum's collections quite recently, since it has been in existence for barely 30 years. But in this period groups of exhibits have been assembled to illustrate such fascinating areas of human endeavour as the artistic working of metals, the history of which is but one example of humankind's timeless quest for beauty. Now, for the first time, our museum is presenting its exhibits in Edinburgh, a city famous for its cultural traditions. We trust that the exhibition will appeal to a wide range of visitors.

Selecting works of art for exhibition beyond the walls of the museum, where they exist in complete collections, is never easy, since the objects may lose their proper context. But from tens of thousands of pieces of jewelry we have attempted to pick out not only the most important but also those which, illustrating some common thread, can help sketch a picture of artistic endeavours in the Ukraine over two millenia.

The most ancient exhibits are in the polychrome style, and demonstrate the quality of artistic workmanship amongst the enigmatic Cimmerians. They are the first tribes known to us by name. They are mentioned in historical sources in connection with the most stirring events of antiquity - the destruction of states and the razing of cities in Asia Minor. Archaeological traces of them are however meagre, and so each find is an invaluable relic of their age.

A large section of the exhibition is devoted to the Scythian culture and to the ancient cities of the northern Black Sea area. Archaeological excavations have been conducted in the Ukraine for over two hundred years. It is thanks to them that many examples of decorative artwork, made 2,500 years ago, have come to light. They command attention, being so striking in their perfection of form and sophistication of metalworking technique. Of all the artefacts that have come out of the Scythian burials, the most outstanding are the ornaments for clothing, weaponry, and the bridles of horses. In the exhibition visitors will see objects made when Scythian culture was at its height in the 4th century BC. They demonstrate the unique artistic styles which came about through the cultural interaction of the local tribes, the newly arrived nomadic Scythians, and the Greek settlers. Visitors will be struck by the amazing work done by the craftsmen of the Greek colonies - earrings, necklaces, torques, and most of all the pectoral. It is not for nothing that it has been called the find of the century. Quite apart from its appeal as an object of beauty, it also contains coded "messages" which reflect the world view of the Scythians.

An interesting page in the history of jewelry was turned at the beginning of the first millenium AD. Medieval tribes, which appeared one after another in the period of the great migrations, have left behind traces of their stay, and objects have been found in their graves which tell of the contacts between peoples and of their manufacturing techniques.

The largest section of the exhibition invites the visitor to become acquainted with the jewelry traditions of Old Rus. In this, one of the most highly developed states of the Middle Ages, the making of jewelry was widespread. Creatively developing their Byzantine legacy, the craftsmen of Old Rus produced pieces of jewelry which are among the masterpieces of the world. Particularly outstanding are the objects decorated with the most delicate partitioned enamelwork. The colours are bright and untarnished - as if confirming the imperishability of true art.This could also be said of the output of Ukrainian jewellers in the 17th and 18th centuries. Whatever storms and turmoil cross the face of the earth, the human endeavour to create beauty triumphs in the end. A striking feature of the pieces dedicated to church use - crosses, tabernacles, dishes, and so on - are the ornamental compositions based on flowers and fruit. They are lavishly brilliant, and give the feeling that these craftsmen were inspired by nature around them.

In concluding this short introduction, I should like to emphasize once more that we have tried to include the most characteristic works from each stage in the development of the Ukraine's jewelry tradition. The unfading glory of their creators can help us to understand more deeply the beauty of the world today, and to value the inspired work of the ancient craftsmen.

Cat. No : 39

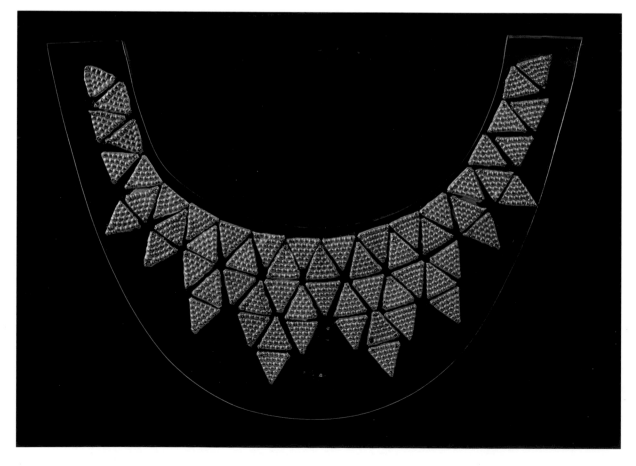

The Northern Black Sea Area in the First millenium B.C.

Many relics of antiquity are preserved in the Ukraine. Among the most outstanding are the barrows, which are earthworks sited over burials. They are one of the most remarkable features of the Ukrainian landscape, particularly the steppe region, the majestic "pyramids of the steppe", as they have been called by academics, poets and travellers. They have always attracted great interest, and so have become surrounded by legends and mystery.

The first of these sites to be excavated - 230 years ago - was the Litaya Mogila barrow, although it became known to archaeologists as the Melgunov site. It marked the beginning of studies of the tribes whose remains have come down to us via these burials. Over two centuries several thousand barrows have been investigated by archaeologists. Each one enables us to feel close to the life of these ancient peoples. In the northern Black Sea area of the first millenium BC, two nations contributed particularly vivid episodes to the historical record - the Cimmerians and the Scythians. Their names we know from the writings of historians who portrayed them as tribes both numerous, and ferocious in battle (Map A).

The Cimmerians are the oldest of the European tribes living north of the Black Sea and Danube, and whom we know by the name they used for themselves. We find the first mention of them in the *Odyssey* and *Iliad* of Homer, and later in Assyrian cuneiform texts from the 8th century BC. Of particular interest is the information given by the "father of history", the Greek historian Herodotus (5th century BC). These isolated glimpses enable us to reconstruct a picture of the events of the first millenium B.C. associated with the legendary Cimmerians and Scythians.

Thus Herodotus writes that the whole of the North Pontic steppe region, occupied in his time by the Scythians, belonged earlier to the Cimmerians. "The Scythians - nomads living in Asia - were driven out by wars with the Massagetae, and came ... to the land of the Cimmerians." Since the incoming armies were more powerful than the local population, the ordinary people decided to abandon the land without putting up any resistance. The kings, on the other hand, resolved "to die, and lie for ever in their own land, not to flee with the rest of the people. When they had made this decision, they divided themselves into two equal armies and joined battle with each other. All of them having died at one another's hands, they were buried by the Cimmerian people at the River Tyras, and the grave can still be seen there to the present day" (Herodotus, IV, 11).

The Cimmerians surged into Asia Minor. This was in the seventies of the 7th century BC. They annihilated the Phrygian kingdom after destroying and looting its capital, Gordium. In 652 BC they captured Sardis and plundered the Greek cities of the Aegean coast and Asia Minor. In the thirties of the 7th century Cimmerian forces were checked and routed by the Assyrians who came to the aid of the Scythians. In the 6th century the name of the Cimmerians disappeared from the historical scene.

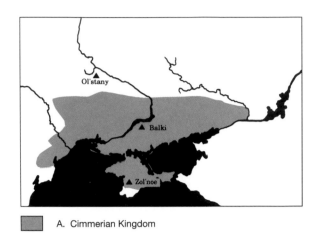

A. Cimmerian Kingdom

Archaeological research shows that the "Cimmerian" period in the history of southern Ukraine began in the late 11th or early 10th century BC. Few remains have been studied in the steppe zone, where in all probability nomads were predominant, though some excavations have been carried out on their burial sites. The population of the forest-steppe, on the other hand, was settled and agricultural. Of particular interest are their settlements, hill forts and burial grounds. Objects found have attracted the interest of specialists in the "Cimmerian culture". They have recorded a diverse, and, for the time, highly developed, set of weapons - swords, spears, battle hammers, and the bow and arrow. It has been established that their quiver held from 30 to 50 arrows, clear evidence for the importance of the bow. Judging by pictorial representations, they were complex and comparatively small, but quite powerful, and intended for mounted archers. A picture of mounted warriors, armed with swords and shooting arrows, is included in a painting on an antique vase (fig.1).

War encourages many trades. The study of iron weaponry has revealed highly developed metal-working techniques. Smiths had methods enabling them to manufacture objects of complex form. Many artefacts were made of bronze, mainly by casting. Particular skill is required in casting the details of horse bridles - the bit, snaffle and small bells. Some examples are real masterpieces of the *cire perdue* casting technique. The construction of the bridles suggests that they were used not only for saddle horses but also for chariots.

Gold ornaments have also been found in the Cimmerians' graves. Included in the exhibition are examples of jewelry in the polychrome style. One is a decorative gold plate made of notched gold wire rings and white glazing paste (cat. no.9). Another provisionally has been called a "pin", but there is another interpretation of it: it is possibly an imitation ceremonial klevets (a pointed hammer for embossing, or trimming millstones), which was a symbol of high social status. It is decorated with blue glass (cat.no.8).

The culture of the society which left behind these relics was highly individual, and had its roots in the later Bronze Age. On the steppes of the Left-bank Ukraine (the area to the east of the Dnieper river) in the 10th-9th centuries BC appeared tribes which, in the opinion of archaeologists, were the first wave of Asiatic nomads. They brought with them new types of dagger, arrow-heads, bits, and so on. But gradually this influx from the east merged into the local scene, although certain features remained until Scythian times. There were apparently considerable similarities between the local inhabitants and the newly arrived "proto-Scythians" in language, clothing, weaponry, and bridles. There is evidence for this in many written sources. At the time of the raids into the Near East the middle eastern peoples of the area did not regard them as separate.

The question arises whether these legendary tribes were of a single racial stock. Most probably not. No one nation in antiquity, lacking a state, would have been able to mount such long-distance and powerful military incursions. It is probable that they were raids or more likely migrations of nomadic tribes which drew after them both whole ethnic communities and separate military forces. However, the core of this invasion was the people bearing the name of Cimmerians, a name which the Greek written tradition clearly associated with the people living on the north coast of the Black Sea.

In the 7th century BC a new wave of Asiatic nomads, known to history as the Scythians, swept over the same area. Let us once more turn to the *Histories* of Herodotus to view these events through his eyes. He records that the Scythians went after the Cimmerians, who fled from them across the Caucasus. "Pursuing the Cimmerians, they invaded Asia, destroying the power of the Medes" (Herodotus, IV, 1). Thus began their raids into the Near

fig. 1

East which continued until the 6th century B.C.

In league with Assyria the Scythians took part in the war against the people of Mannai, under the leadership of Ishpakai. Despite this, the Scythians soon afterwards became allies of Mannai against Assyria. With their help the state of Urartu was destroyed. Being unsurpassed as archers and courageous warriors they advanced as far as Syria, where the Egyptian pharoah Psammetichus bought them off with gifts. The Scythians held sway in Asia Minor for 28 years (652 - 625 B.C.), laying it waste by excessive tributes and plundering. This was brought to an end when "Cyaxares and the Medes invited the greater number of them to a feast, made them exceedingly drunk, and slaughtered them" (Herodotus, I, 106).

"After suffering defeat, the Scythians returned to their own country" (Herodotus, IV, 1). It is likely that this refers to the steppes of both the northern Caucasus and the Black Sea area. The northern Caucasus was the natural launching pad for the raids into the Near East. Here the Scythians returned after their defeat, and became the dominant power in the area. Evidence of this is seen in their numerous barrows, unique in their size and the richness of the tombs. In some barrows distinctive trophies of the raids into the Near East have been found - for example, jewelry showing eastern workmanship was discovered in the Melgunov barrow mentioned earlier. It is possible that a distinguished participant of the famous raids was buried there.

In the late 7th or early 6th century B.C., the forest-steppe regions along the River Dnieper were incorporated into Scythia. These were inhabited by agricultural tribes. Most likely the force of arms had something to do with it.... Herodotus relates how the Scythians, having returned from Asia, endured a great war in their homeland "no less than that with the Medes". Resisting the Scythians were the children born to their wives, who had been left behind during the raids, and slaves. "Having discovered the circumstances of their birth, they resolved to offer resistance to those returning from the country of the Medes". The Scythians were not able to prevail on the field of battle, so they decided to throw away their spears and bows and take up instead horse whips, for "so long as they see us using weapons they consider themselves like us and our equals. But as soon as they see whips and not weapons in our hands they will understand that they are our slaves, and realising that they will not stand their ground" (Herodotus, IV, 3). It turned out as the Scythians had supposed; the slaves "lost their wits ... forgot about the battle, and turned to flee" (Herodotus, IV, 4) Undoubtedly this passage reflects events connected with the Scythian conquest of large areas of the northern Black Sea area.

Almost at the same time as the Scythians appeared in the Black Sea area, settlers arrived from Greece and Asia Minor (Ionia)to establish colonies on the Black Sea coast. In Hellas at this time conditions existed which forced many people to emigrate, and some of these sought out fertile land and trade opportunities. Many did this on account of the wars with the Persians.

The coastal areas were not occupied by settled populations, and so the Greeks rapidly occupied extensive territories without any hindrance. Having founded colonial cities with such attractive names as Olbia (meaning 'happy'), Theodosia and Panticapaeum, the Greek settlers entered into close relations with their neighbours, the "barbarians" (which is what the Greeks called all non-Greeks).

The Greek settlers brought their own culture, which influenced all aspects of life in the city colonies. Science, art, and trades were all developed. As we shall see later, in the northern Black Sea area there was an interaction between the cultures of many different peoples settled in the region, and as a result there arose a very rich, unique and distinctive culture in which were interwoven the traditions of Greeks, Scythians and other peoples. Thanks to the great interest the Greeks showed in their neighbours, we can see the Scythians through their eyes. Herodotus visited Olbia in the 5th century. He probably met Scythians, heard their legends, and inquired about their customs.

According both to Herodotus and the archaeological evidence, the Scythians occupied territory from the Danube to the Don. The northern boundary is fixed only very provisionally, on the basis of excavations of their remains: it was approximately at the latitude of Kiev. Near Olbia lived the Callipidae and Graeco-Scythians, and farther north the Alazones. These and others led a Scythian way of life, even though they grew cereals, millet, onions, garlic and lentils. The population between the Dnieper and Dniester was of "ploughmen-Scythians", who produced grain for sale. "If you cross the Boristhenes [as the Greeks called the Dnieper], the country next to the sea is Hylaea, and going farther north you come to the country where dwell the agricultural Scythians [Borisphenites]" (Herodotus, IV, 18).

East of the agricultural Scythians lived nomadic Scythians: "these nomads inhabit ... the country stretching to the River Gerrhus" (Herodotus, IV, 19). And here is one of the enigmas of Herodotus: experts are still unable to agree which river is meant. It is important to know, if we are to determine where "live the bravest and most numerous of the Scythians, who regard the other Scythians as their slaves". According to Herodotus the River Gerrhus was the border between the nomadic Scythians and the Royal Scythians. Some experts have suggested that the land of the nomadic Scythians was located on the steppes along the Dnieper, while farther east, as far as Palus Maeotis (the Sea of Azov), lived the Royal Scythians (map B).

The Scythians spoke an Iranian language. The original area in which Iranian was spoken extended from the mid-Volga and the Don regions to the northern Urals and beyond. From here Iranian-speaking tribes colonised Media, Parthia, Persia, Central Asia and as far as the Chinese border. The appearance of the Scythians in the 7th century BC in the northern Black Sea area was as one of the waves bringing Iranian-speaking tribes to Eastern Europe. These movements of peoples were very complex, but in very broad terms we can say that the nomadic and agricultural Scythians comprised the northern branch of the Iranian peoples, while the "ploughmen" Scythians were probably proto-Slavs.

With the creation of the enormous Scythian state, all the tribes participating in it, as well as neighbouring ones, began a new phase of their history. Relations with the Greeks were peaceful, and regulated by agreements. Herodotus describes in some detail the country inhabited by the Scythians. It was characterised by rich pastures and full rivers. The Borysthenes (Dnieper) "provides the herds with excellent and very nutritious grazing, a great abundance of magnificent fish, and sweet-tasting water whose clarity makes a contrast with the turbid waters of other Scythian rivers. Along it stretches outstanding farmland, while tall grass grows where the plough is not used. At the mouth of the river salt accumulates by itself, and from the estuary are caught large spineless fish for salting, and these are called sturgeon. Besides all this there is much else to wonder at" (Herodotus, IV, 53).

The nomadic Scythians occupied the steppe region of modern Ukraine, where they raised horses and sheep. They wandered with their herds across the country looking for pasture. These migrations were regular and organised, to north or south according to the season. "No-one confronting them can escape on foot, and if they wish not to be discovered it is impossible to engage with them. The reason is that they do not build towns or fortresses, but all of them are mounted archers and carry their homes with them, living in their waggons, and gain their sustenance not from the plough but from raising domestic animals. How can they fail to be invincible, and immune from attack?" (Herodotus, IV, 46).

As we see, this is a comprehensive description. By contrast Herodotus said rather little about those who gained their living from the plough. Why? Perhaps because he considered that "the Pontus Euxinus [Black Sea] ... in comparison with all other countries is inhabited by the most uncivilised nations, with the exception of the Scythians" (Herodotus, IV, 46).

Archaeological research shows, however, that the areas settled by the agricultural tribes were highly developed both economically and culturally. Here there were hill forts and settlements in which were manufactured metal tools, weapons, and ornaments, while from them there was an active trade with the Greek colonies and with their neighbours to the west. There was a large export of grain from the Right-bank Ukraine to Greece via the colonies, and this also suggests a highly developed economy.

The agricultural and nomadic Scythians coexisted in one state. And it was probably not for nothing that Herodotus emphasized that some of the Scythians regarded the rest as their slaves, that is; subjects or more exactly tributaries.

There is one reason why the "father of history" gave so much detailed information about the Scythians; he wanted to describe the people who had succeeded in defeating the Persian king Darius. This was a most important episode in the history of the Scythians, and the memory of it remained with them for many years. Darius I crossed the Bosphorus and invaded Scythia. The Scythians had however devised an unusual tactic for conducting warfare. The Persians expected to crush the Scythians in a decisive engagement, but the latter avoided such a battle. They retreated deep into their territory, laying waste the region and wearing down the enemy by means of small raids. In pursuing the Scythians Darius soon came to appreciate the cunning of these "partisan" tactics. Reaching the Volga, Darius, acknowledging defeat, had to retreat from Scythia in shame.

The Scythians were always waging small wars. It is known, for instance, that they regularly carried out raids against the Sindi along the River Kuban, crossing the Cimmerian Bosphorus (Kerch Strait) on the ice (Herodotus, IV, 28). In 496 BC they raided beyond the Danube as far as Thracian Chersonesus on the Sea of Marmara.

Even during the raids into the Near East, the Scythians had a state of their own. It is likely that after the raids the Scythians were organised as several large tribal alliances, each ruled by a king. Describing the war between the Scythians and the Persians, Herodotus names three kings, the chief of whom was Idanthyrsus. It is probable that in the 4th century BC a single autocracy was set up. There is written evidence for this in the case of King Atheas. In the words of the Roman historian Strabo, "It seems that Atheas rules over most of the barbarians in this region". At this time Scythia acquired great power, and evidence for this consists in the appearance of coinage; several gold coins have survived on which is portrayed a mounted archer holding a bow, and bearing the name 'Atheas'. It was a symbol of a unified state and a unique declaration of its power.

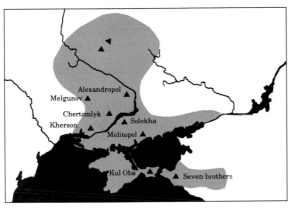

B. Distribution of Scythian "Royal" tombs

King Atheas strived to extend the boundaries of his state. Scythian power reached beyond the Danube, to the lands of Thracian tribes. Scythia was prevented from extending beyond the Danube by Macedonia, which occupied the north-eastern part of the Balkan peninsula. In 339 BC, a great battle took place between the Scythians, led by the 90-year-old Atheas, and the Macedonians under the supreme command of Philip II (the father of the celebrated Alexander the Great), in which the Scythian forces were defeated and King Atheas was killed. But even after this the struggle between Scythia and Macedonia continued. In 331 BC, Alexander's second-in-command Zopyrion attacked Olbia with a large force. The town withstood a siege and the 30,000 strong army of Zopyrion was defeated by the Scythians. In 292 BC the Scythians, in alliance with Thracian tribes of Goths, routed the forces of Lysimachus, the ruler of Thrace.

However, in the 3rd century BC Scythian power declined significantly. There were several causes, the main one probably being ecological. It is evident the natural and climatic conditions of life on the steppe were changing. According to some experts there was a "desertification" of the steppe. The population moved to more favourable areas, in particular southwards to the southern Dnieper. Greater Scythia disintegrated in the late 3rd century BC, and the territory now only extended from the Lower Dnieper to the Crimea. The town called Neapolis became the capital of the new state; it was located on the River Salgir, and near it Simferopol later grew up. One other territory remained under Scythian control, near Dobruja beyond the Danube. The Scythians appear even later in written sources. They are mentioned more than once up to the 3rd century AD, when they finally succumbed to attacks from the Goths. The history of the Scythians, stretching over almost a thousand years, is stamped on what they have left behind - not only in tangible remains but also in cultural influences.

So let us return to the barrows. Excavations of them have shown that the name "steppe pyramids" given them by travellers and specialists is not merely a fanciful analogy with the tombs of the Egyptian pharaohs. They have revealed one of their chief characteristics, namely that they were indeed like the Egyptian pyramids in being complex and labour-consuming constructions. They were raised as clay or earth embankments, with the slopes strengthened with soft clay. Each barrow has its own peculiarities: sometimes the surface is covered with a stone "shell", and the foundation may be of limestone slabs.

The height of the "steppe pyramids" closely reflected the status of their inhabitant when alive. Some are as high as 20 metres, and these have been provisionally called "royal barrows". Sometimes two or three methods were used to build them. The details of their construction can be worked out thanks to the careful manner in which they have been studied. A bulldozer is used to dig trenches through the barrow, and of particular importance are the sections revealed on the sides of the trenches. The sections reveal the stages in the building of the barrow.

It is clear from the descriptions given earlier that the Scythian population had different ethnic origins, and this is also seen in their burial rites. Thus, in the forest-steppe regions, they buried their dead in wooden tombs.

In the corners of the pit tree trunks were set up, the walls and floor were made of planks, and the roof consisted of one or two layers of beams. The nomadic Scythians on the steppe buried their dead in underground catacombs. They first dug out an entrance hole, and in one wall excavated a distinctive kind of cave-catacomb. This is the general layout, but no two burials are exactly alike (fig.2).

The catacombs in the "royal" barrows are enormous subterranean constructions. They comprise a deep entrance with steps, an entrance to the dromos (entrance passage), and a room 2-2.5 metres high with convenient recesses in the walls. Seeing this you cannot help being astonished by the engineering skills of those ancient builders.

All archaeologists experience a rare feeling when, after much hard, painstaking work, they at last have the opportunity to penetrate the burial chamber. And although there remains a great deal more work to be done, this first step into the catacomb takes the archaeologists back into Scythian times. On the floor is laid out the dead person, in ceremonial attire with the obligatory assemblage of grave artefacts. In women's graves these are pottery, distaff, and spindles, and in men's pride of place is given to the weapons - swords, javelins, spears, and quivers with arrows. Often horses with all their accoutrements were buried with the men.

The grave goods were selected in accordance with the material wealth and social position of the dead person. They reflected the religious, aesthetic and moral norms of the time. Every object is a valuable document of the epoch and tells a great deal about the life of the Scythians (fig. 3.).

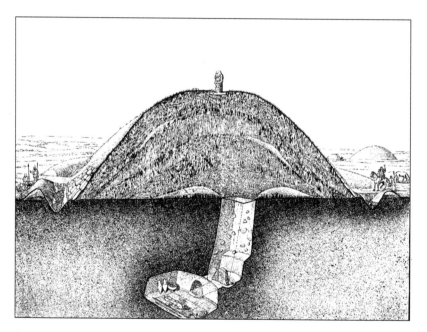

fig. 2 : Diagram of a Scythian tomb: section of a barrow, and its general structure.

Herodotus noted the burial customs of the Scythians. "When they bury a king, they dig a large rectangular hole in the ground. When it is ready, they take the corpse, rub it with wax, remove the internal organs, fill the cleaned out abdomen with crushed galingale, aniseed, parsley-seeds, and perfume, sew it up, and then carry it on a waggon to another tribe". All the tribes subject to the Scythians were given the chance to say farewell to the king and to express their grief: "they cut off parts of their ears, shave their heads, and make incisions on their arms". The burial site was in the country of the Gerrhi, "on the very edge of the territory". They strangled and buried with the king "one of his concubines, his cup-bearer, cook, groom, steward, herald, and also his horses and a selection of everything else. Having done all this, they erect a great barrow" (Herodotus, IV, 71).

So far archaeologists have not found an answer to the question of where the kings' necropolis was located, or in other words the land of the Gerrhi. "Royal" barrows which have been investigated in the steppe belong to the 4th century BC. But what of the earlier ones? This is still a mystery (one of many).

Herodotus heard two legends about the Scythians' ancestors. One was from the Scythians and the other from the Greeks. "This is what the Scythians say about themselves ... The first man on the earth ... was called Targitaus. The parents of this Targitaus were ... Zeus and the daughter of the River Borysthenes. This was the origin of Targitaus. He had three sons - Leipoxais, Arpoxais, and the youngest who was Coloxais. During their reign over Scythia there were cast down from heaven certain objects of gold: a plough with a yoke, a double-edged battle axe, and a dish. Being the first to see them, the eldest came up with the intention of taking them, but on his approach the gold burst into flames. After he had retreated the second son came up, but once more the gold caught fire. When the third and youngest son went up to the gold, the fire went out and he took up the objects.

After this the older sons agreed to hand all royal power to the youngest" (Herodotus, IV, 5). Coloxais gave rise to a line of kings, and was regarded as the Scythian hero-ancestor. It is likely that representations of him have survived in stone sculptures. They are large limestone statues of a man holding weapons and a rhyton. Several objects included in the grave inventory probably reflect the cult of the hero-ancestor, in particular the rhyton, and drinking vessels (cat.nos.29, 30, 31)

"But the Greeks living near the Black Sea relate the following story. Heracles ... came to this land which was at the time deserted but is now occupied by the Scythians.... Here he was overtaken by winter and frost, and drawing about him his lion-skin cloak he fell asleep, but his horses ... were mysteriously spirited away.... When Heracles awoke, he set out to search for them. Traversing the whole land, he eventually came to a country called Hylaea. Here he found in a cave a dual creature, half viper and half woman; above the buttocks a maiden, and below a serpent.... Heracles slept with her.... When she gave back his horses she said to him, 'I have kept your horses for you, which wandered here, and for this you have given me my reward, for you see that I have by you

three sons. Tell me what I should do with them when they are grown to be men'.... And he replied, '... When you see that one of them can draw this bow as I show you, and girdle himself with this belt as I do, he may make this country his home....' When they were grown up, she first gave them their names, one Agathyrsus, the next Gelonus, and the youngest Scythes.... Scythes, having fulfilled the tasks, remained in the country. And from Scythes, the son of Heracles, descended the present kings of the Scythians" (Herodotus, IV, 10).

Isolated episodes of these legends are depicted in magnificent examples of Greek jewelry, in particular in a richly decorated cover of a gorytus (cat.no.25). The image of the goddess Api, found on gold ornaments, also originated in the art of the northern Black Sea area (cat.no.54). Articles made of precious metals which archaeologists find in graves are striking, and also impressive in their technical accomplishment. They more than

fig. 3 : Grave goods from an original Scythian burial site.

any other discoveries open a window onto the world of the Scythians since they have the ability to provide an unusual amount of information. Gold ornaments were commissioned by the Scythians to be made in the workshops of the Greek colonies, and those in Panticapaeum and Olbia were particularly adept at making jewelry. In the 4th century BC various styles and trends in representational art emerged through the medium of ornaments.

But let us return to the early history of the Scythians in the Black Sea area. The immigrant tribes of nomadic herdsmen brought to this area elements from their own culture, known as the "Scythian triad" - weaponry, bridles, and the animal style. Generally speaking the "animal style" means the representation of animals in certain poses - with their legs drawn in and the head turned. These ancient artists were able to combine in one composition both realism and a high degree of simplification, both detail and the generic idea. Despite the static pose, which is called "sacrificial" since the legs of sacrificial animals are bound in the same way, they were able to give the impression of the animal being alive. One specialist, G.N.Borovka, has called it "primitive impressionism".

The earliest motifs in Scythian art, common to the whole Eurasian area, are deer, horses, and feline beasts of prey. The forest zone gave Scythian art the images of the elk, bear, and canine beasts of prey. And ancient far eastern art contributed the griffin and various monsters. The problem of how to interpret these images has still not been settled. One suggestion is that the animals are incarnations or embodiments of various gods and heroes. But at the same time one god may have several different forms. For instance, the sun god might take the form of a deer, or a horse, or an elk.

From a very early stage, one of the images used by the Scythians on a variety of artefacts was the griffin. A mythical creature with the body of a lion and the head and wings of an eagle appeared in art as early as the 2nd millenium BC, in the Creto-Mycenaean culture. The Scythians probably acquired it during their sojourn in the Near East. Various concepts have been attached to the image of the griffin. According to the Scythians it was a creature which united the upper world (the heavenly) and the lower (the earthly). Besides, the griffin possessed magical and protective powers (cat.nos.45 & 46).

Geometrical patterns were also characteristic of early Scythian art - concentric circles and triangles composed of rings. They are ancient solar symbols. The triangle also has a deeper meaning. In many cultures it signifies the unity of three elements - earth, water, and air. In addition, the triangle standing on a point indicates the female principle, while one standing on a side symbolises the male principle.

In this system of imagery - the "animal" motifs and the geometrical patterns - ancient artistic traditions became more and more interwoven. Greek art contributed the images of the wild boar and the lion (cat.nos.32, 44). Vegetation patterns and the representation of humans also appeared.

From now on, the Scythian gods took on a human form. We can turn once more to Herodotus, to the passage in which he gives the names of the Scythian gods. This enables us to link the gods with the images: "Among the gods they revered only these: before all others Hestia, and then Zeus and Earth (believing that Earth was the wife of Zeus), and after them Apollo and Celestial Aphrodite, Heracles and Ares. All Scythians hold these gods sacred. Those Scythians which are called Royal also sacrifice to Poseidon. The Scythian name for Hestia is Tabiti, Zeus ... is Papaeus, Earth is Api, Apollo is Oetosyrus, Celestial Aphrodite is Argimpasa, and Poseidon is Thagimasadas. They do not erect statues, nor altars, nor temples to any of the gods except to Ares" (Herodotus, IV, 50).

Of all these gods and goddesses, it is clear only what Api looked like - with the legs of a serpent and bats' wings (cat.no.54). As for the others, Greek iconography comes to our aid. Thus Celestial Aphrodite may be recognised by her mirror. Among the gold decorative plaques with images in relief are those on which a scene is depicted inside a frame: on a stool sits a woman in a magnificent costume, with a mirror in her hand. In front of her is a Scythian with a rhyton which he is raising to his lips. It is assumed that this depicts Argimpasa who probably, like Aphrodite, had a mirror as her main distinguishing characteristic. Argimpasa was regarded as the patron of the Scythian kings. This striking composition reflects the Scythians' idea of their kings' divine protection. The scene has been called "adoration" or supplication (cat.nos.50, 51).

Gold decorative plaques bear patterns, images and motifs which reflect the cult of fertility. It was the principal religious concern among ancient peoples. And it is understandable, since if the community was to survive, the birth of children had to be taken seriously. Also it was the key to prosperity in the form of the fruits of agriculture and animal-breeding. Effort and prayer were directed to these ends. Thus all the images - of plants, animals and people - represented a unique form of magical appeal or prayer.

Most of the gold objects were intended as decoration for men and women. Scythian ceremonial costume looked sumptuous. Head-dresses, clothing and footwear were embroidered in gold. The shapes of all these can be reconstructed from depictions and from archaeological finds.

The male image is particularly expressively conveyed in surviving decorative metalworks. Man is glorified in art, and his heroic and manly characteristics are emphasized (fig.4). Clothing is rendered in detail, with the seams picked out by means of patterns. Jackets and trousers were probably sewn from leather and cloth. They fitted the figure well and were distinguished by their comfort, simplicity, and the practical means of making them (fig.5). A man's ceremonial costume included removable ornaments - torques and rings. The material these were made from and the skill of the jeweller reflected the status of the owner. For instance, a torque ending in little lions' heads and with enamalled patterns indicated that the owner was from the artistocratic elite (cat.no.34).

fig.4 : Tracing of a relief on a gold plaque. From the Kul-oba barrow, excavated 1830.

One of the most outstanding achievements of the Panticapaeum jewellers is a pectoral (cat.no.64). It was a decoration worn on the chest, a symbol of royal power, and possibly also with sacred functions which were the prerogative of the king. This was a feature commonly found in ancient societies.

There are also depictions of female attire, but as we shall see they were rather schematic (cat.nos.38, 50, 51). Archaeological material helps to complete the details and to reveal the significance of some of them. Using all these sources together we can picture the Scythian woman in all her finery. It was an effective combination of rich fabrics and gold trimmings. Its meaning was expressed in the form and decoration of the head-dresses - the ribbons, hats, and shawls. Most significant of these were the hats. They were tall and firm, since they were intended to display patterns which were symbols of the gods of fertility in nature. Two shapes were characteristic - cylindrical (cat.no.37) and conical (cat.no.36). They showed the social and family status of the owner.

The women's upper garments were robes, dresses and jackets. A robe emphasized the wearer's aristocratic superiority. One short, loose jacket with fur trimming stands out on account of its exaggeratedly elongated sleeves. The clear outline in a dress was created by the so-called tunic-shaped pattern made from two or three pieces of cloth. In contrast to the robes they were comfortable and practical, while at the same time looking smart and showing off the figure.

The favourite ornament of Scythian women was the earring. The so-called "kalachiki" each in the shape of a small white loaf, attract particular attention. This is a very ancient type, originating in the East and becoming widely disseminated in Asia Minor and Greece. In Scythia it was modified in accordance with local taste, and pendants appeared in the form of little ducks. They are a symbol of fertility, and the earrings became the fashion among young women (fig. 6; cat.no.53).

Neck ornaments included torques (cat.no.41) and necklaces, and these completed the symbolism of the costume since their motifs predominantly reflected the cult of fertility. An example is a string of gold beads shaped like fruit with lunar pendants (cat.no.40). Jewelry for the hand (bracelets and rings) were mainly symbols of protection. If made of gold, they expressed the social distinction of the wearer (cat.nos.60-63). Ancient centres renowned for their artefacts continued to make a variety of orna-

fig. 5 : Reconstructed male Scythian costume.

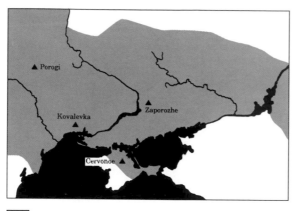

C. Sarmatian Culture

ments even after Greater Scythia had dissolved. There was a demand for them not only in the Greek colonies (cat.nos.72-74) but also among the barbarians (cat.nos. 66-70).

At the end of the 2nd century BC there began a massive influx of Sarmatian tribes into the Black Sea steppe. They brought in different traditions and aesthetic ideas. In particular they favoured using turquoise and gold (cat.no. 65). A new page had been turned in the cultural history of the area (map C).

The objects displayed in the exhibition illustrate some of the most important stages in the development of the applied arts in antiquity. They represent a distillation of both the technical achievements and the spiritual values of the society of which they were a product.

fig. 6 : Earrings with pendants. 4th c. BC.

TRIPOLSKI CULTURE

1. UPPER PORTION OF STATUETTE OF A WOMAN.

Last quarter of the 3rd millenium BC
Clay, paint. Modelled.
70 x 45 x 30mm.
Settlement, Vladimirovka village,
Podvuisotskii area,
Kirovogradskaya district.
Excavated by T.S. Passek, 1940.
NHMU, inv. No. a26/2440.

Perhaps of religious significance.

CATACOMB CULTURE

2. MACE HEAD.

2000 - 1600 BC
Marble, stone. Carved, polished.
Diameter 62mm, height 53mm.
Burial mound, town of Svatovo,
Luganskaya district.
Excavated by S.N. Bratchenko,
1974.
NMHU inv. No. a377.

3-4. ASTRAGALI (DICE)

2000 - 1600 c. BC
Sheep's vertebrae. Polished.
37 x 25mm, 34 x 25mm.
Burial mound, town of Svatovo,
Luganskaya district.
Excavated by S.N. Bratchenko,
1974.
NMHU inv. ad204.

*"Astragali" appear to have had
some religious significance and
were frequently buried with the
dead.*

5-7. BLOCKS FOR PLAYING DICE.

2000 - 1600 BC
Bone. Carved, polished.
10 x 12 x 8mm.
Burial mound, town of Svatovo,
Luganskaya district.
Excavated by S.N. Bratchenko,
1974.
NMHU inv. No. a379-381.

8

CIMMERIAN

9

8. PIN (?)

8th c. BC
Gold, earthenware, glass. Forged,
drawn wire, filigree, inlaid work.
Length - 78mm
Burial mound, village of Olshani,
Gorodishenskii area,
Cherkasskaya district.
Excavated by G.T. Kovpanenko,
1984.
MHTU inv. No. AZS-3774.

*Perhaps a religious artefact. Its
shape suggests that it may have
been used as the top of a staff.*

9. DECORATIVE GOLD PLATE

8th c. BC
Gold, silver, earthenware. Forged, engraved, inlaid work.
Diameter - 36mm.
Burial mound, Balki village, Vasilyevski area, Zaporozhskaya district.
Excavated by V.I. Bidzili, 1971.
MHTU, inv. No. AZS-2676.

Probably a mounting from the strap of a sword-belt.

SCYTHIAN

10. HATCHET-SHAPED STAFF.

7th - 6th c. BC
Bronze. Cast.
310 x 75mm.
Place and date of discovery unknown.
From the collection of B.I. and V.N. Khanenko.
NMHU, inv. No. B 2336.

Anthropomorphic. Possibly had religious significance.

11. POLE TOP

7th - 6th c. BC
Bronze. Cast.
Length - 170mm; Height - 55mm; Width - 30mm.
Place and date of discovery unknown.
NMHU, inv. No.B 2699.

Artefacts such as this have been found across Mesopotamia. Most often they had religious significance.

12. BELT BUCKLE

7th - 5th c. BC
Bronze. Cast.
95 x 95mm.
Tsea village, North Ossetia, Caucasus.
Date of discovery unknown.
NMHU, inv. No. B 2698.

Ornamented with the image of a deer with spreading antlers.

12

13. PLAQUES IN FORM OF A STAG

First half of 6th c. BC
Gold. Stamped.
40 x 33mm.
Burial mound, Sinyavka village, Kanevksi area, Cherkasskaya district.
Excavated by Y.A. Znosko-Borovski, 1897.
MHTU, inv. No. DM-6307/2,3.

The image of the deer (one of the most popular in Scythian art) is linked to the cult of the sun. These plaques would have decorated ceremonial garments.

14. PLAQUES IN THE FORM OF A HORSE

First half of 6th c. BC
Gold. Stamped.
40 x 27mm.
Burial mound, Bobritsi village, Kanevski area, Cherkasskaya district.
Excavated by Y.A. Znosko-Borovski, 1897
MHTU, inv. No. AZS-988/3,8.

15. POLE TOP

6th c. BC
Bronze, iron. Cast, forged.
165 x 60mm.
Burial mound, Budka village, Romenski area, Sumskaya district.
Excavated by S.A. Mazaraki, 1883-1885.
NMHU, inv. No. B33-56.

16. POLE TOP

6th c. BC
Bronze, iron. Cast, forged.
160 x 65mm.
Burial mound, Budka village, Romenski area, Sumskaya district.
Excavated by S.A. Mazaraki, 1883-1885.
NMHU, inv. No. B 30-216.

13

17. POLE TOP

6th c. BC.
Bronze. Cast.
Length - 232mm; diameter -
60mm.
Burial mound, Romenski area,
Sumskaya district.
Excavated by D.Y. Samokvasova,
after 1886.
NMHU, inv. No. B41-425.

*This piece belongs to an early
group of objects made by the
tribes of the forest - steppe. It
apparently had been fastened to a
wagon or chariot.*

18. POLE TOP

6th c. BC
Bronze. Cast.
Length - 232mm; diameter -
60mm.
Burial mound, Romenski area,
Sumskaya district.
Excavated by D.Y. Samokvasova,
after 1886.
NMHU, inv. No. B41-426.

19. POLE TOP

5th c. BC
Bronze, iron. Cast, forged.
Height - 149mm. Length of rod -
126mm. Diameter - 68mm.
Burial mound Volkovtsa village,
Romenski area, Sumskaya district.
Excavated by S.A. Mazaraki,
1897-1898.
NMHU, inv. No. B 32 - 100.

*Pole tops such as this were often
found in graves in pairs. Possibly
symbols of power or may have
been fastened to military or funeral
chariots.*

20. DECORATIVE PLATES FROM SWORD SCABBARD

Turn of the 6th - 5th c. BC
Gold, enamel. Relief stamped,
granulated, filigree, enamelled on
filigree ornamentation.
Tip of the scabbard - 305 x 65-
70mm.
Side blade - 180 x 93mm.
Burial mound, Aleksandrovka vil-
lage, Novomoskovski area,
Dnepropetrovskaya district.
Excavated by N.F. Kovalevoi,
1977.
MHTU, inv. No. AZS-3349-3350.

*The image of the wild boar is rare
among artefacts from this period.
It symbolized one of the incarnations of the Iranian god of thunder
and victory.*

21. "VORVARKA" (METAL CLIP FOR MOUNTING A STRAP OR THONG)

Turn of the 6th - 5th c. BC
Gold. Cast, forged.
Height - 62mm. Lower diameter -
125 x 116mm.
Burial mound, Aleksandrovka vil-
lage, Novomoskovski area,
Dnepropetrovskaya district.
Excavated by N.F. Kovalevoi,
1977.
MHTU, inv. No. AZS - 3352.

17 & 18

Cover for a Gorytus (Cat. No. : 25)

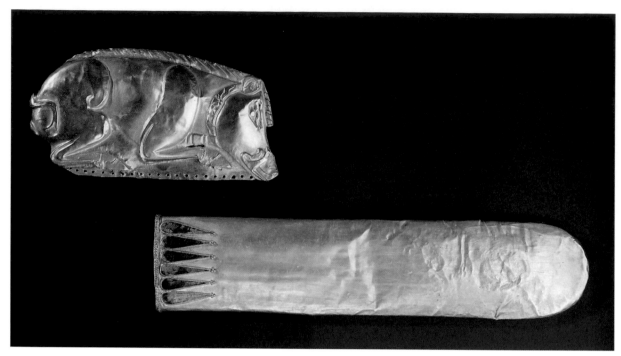

22. SWORD WITH RICHLY ORNAMENTED HILT AND SCABBARD

Middle of 4th c. BC
Iron, gold. Forged, stamped, embossed.
Length of sword - 615mm; length of scabbard - 542mm.
Tolstaya Mogila burial mound, town of Ordzhonkidze, Dnepropetrovskaya district.
Excavated by B.N. Mozolevskii, 1971.
MHTU, inv. No. AZS-2491-2493.

The subjects depicted on the scabbard symbolized life and death. This shape of blade first appeared on artefacts from the end of the 5th c .BC.

23. SWORD WITH RICHLY ORNAMENTED HILT AND SCABBARD.

Last third of 4th c. BC
Iron, gold. Forged, stamped, embossed.
Length - 655mm.
Burial mound, Velikaya Belozerka village, Kamensko-Dneprovski area,
Zaporozhskaya district.
Excavated by V.V. Otroshenko, 1979.
MHTU, inv. No. AZS-3261-3262.

24. DECORATIVE PLATES FROM A GORYTUS

5th c. BC
Gold. Embossed.
85 x 45mm; 96 x 42mm; 63 x 33mm; 40 x 31mm.
Burial mound, Archangelskaya Sloboda village, Kaxovski area, Khersonskaya district.
Excavated by A.M. Leskova, 1969.
MHTU, inv. No. AZS-2325-2328.

Used to ornament a gorytus (a wood and leather container for a bow and arrows).

25. COVER FOR A GORYTUS

4th c. BC
Gold. Embossed.
470 x 230 - 275mm.
Melitopolski burial mound, town of Melitopol, Zaporozhskaya district.
Excavated by A.I. Terenozhnika, 1954.
MHTU, inv. No. AZS-1416.

This richly ornamented cover for a gorytus would have been part of the weaponry of a very high rank-ing Scythian. This particular example relates to others found in the Ukraine, all of them apparently made from the same wooden mould. The decorative friezes depict scenes from the life of Achilles, a hero of the Trojan war. They begin with the young Achilles being taught how to shoot from a bow, and end with his mother Thetis in mourning holding the ashes of her son.

The symbolism is clear. Achilles was killed by a single arrow shot into the only vulnerable part of his body, his heel. In the same way, it was supposed that an arrow taken from this gorytus would slay even the mightiest of enemies.

22

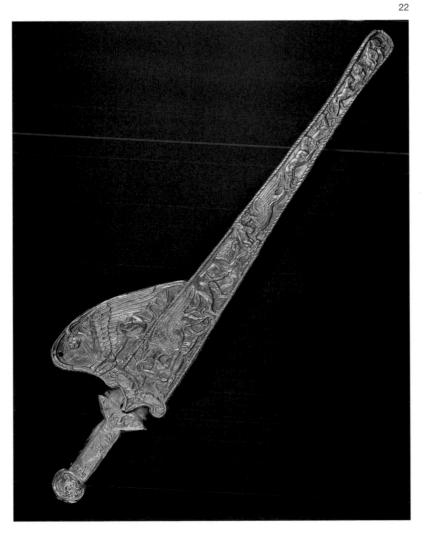

26. PART OF HORSE'S HARNESS, IN THE SHAPE OF A FISH.

4th c. BC
Gold. Embossed.
284 x 45mm.
Burial mound, Volkovtsi village, Romenski area, Sumskaya district.
Excavated by S.A. Mazaraki, 1897-1898.
MHTU inv. No. DM-1708.

Intended to decorate the frontlet of a horse's bridle. Possibly linked with the worship of "Tagimassad", the Scythian god of the sea.

27. ORNAMENTATION FROM A HORSE'S HARNESS.

4th c. BC
Gold, bronze. Cast, stamped.
Berdyanski burial mound, town of Berdyansk, Zaporozhskaya district.
Excavated by N.N. Cherednichenko, 1978-1979.
MHTU, inv. No. AZS-3063, 3065/1-2, 3071/1-4, 3072/1-2.

28. RECONSTRUCTION OF CLOTHING AND WEAPONS OF A SCYTHIAN WARRIOR.

Based on originals dated 5th - 4th c. BC
Leather, iron, wood, bronze, horsehair, fabric. Forged, embossed, sewn, embroidered.
Mailshirt - 1120 x 540mm.
Armour-clad breeches - 710 x 690mm.
Helmet - height 390mm.
Spear - length 2000mm.
Sword - length 510mm.
Based on materials excavated from the burial mound of Gladkovshina village, Cherkasskaya district.
Excavated by V.P. Grigoryeva, 1962.
MHTU, inv. No. TV-2605.

Reconstructed by A.I. Minzhulin, 1990.

29. RHYTON

5th - 4th c. BC
Covering: Gold, organic materials.
Embossed, filigree.
Rhyton (reconstructed) - Length 445mm; diameter of mouth - 135mm.
Burial mound, Velikaya Znamenka village, Kamensko-Dneprovski area, Zaporozhskaya district.
Excavated by V.V. Ostroshenko, 1984.
MHTU, inv. No. AZS-3587.

A vessel in the shape of a horn, the rhyton was made of wood, plated with silver. The wood and silver did not survive but the nine ornamental gold plates around the funnel-shaped opening are original.

30. DRINKING VESSEL

5th c. BC
Covering: Gold, wood.
Embossed.
Drinking vessel (reconstructed) - height 15mm; diameter 115mm.
Plates - 145 x 28mm; 30 x 35mm.
Burial mound, Velikaya Znamenka village, Kamensko-Dneprovski area, Zaporozhskaya district.
Excavated by V.V. Otroshenko, 1984.
MHTU, inv. No. AZS-3583/1-7; NDF-2604/4.

This reconstructed vessel would have had religious significance. The ornamented gold plates are original.

23 (detail)

31. DRINKING VESSEL

4th c. BC
Gold, wood. Embossed.
Drinking vessel (reconstructed) -
Cup - height 90mm; diameter
136mm.
Plates - 69 x 48mm; 67.5 x
47.5mm; 66 x 49mm; 66 x 48mm.
Berdyanski burial mound, town of
Berdyansk, Zaporozhskaya dis-
trict.
Excavated by N.N.
Cherednichenko, 1977-1978.
MHTU, inv. No. AZS-3067/1-4, NDF-2604/2.

*The curve of the plates indicate
that the original vessel was formed
from a single piece of wood. The
ornamented gold plates are original.*

32. FIGURE OF WILD BOAR.

4th c. BC
Gold, silver. Cast, engraved.
Length -50mm; height -28mm.
Burial mound Khomina Mogila,
Nagornoye village, Nikopolski
area, Dnepropetrovskaya district.
Excavated by B.N. Mozolevskii.
1970
MHTU, inv. No. AZS-2451.

*This unique example of ancient
craftsmanship was originally a
handle for a wooden vessel.*

33. TORQUE

5th c. BC
Gold, enamel. Forged, punched,
granulated, enamelled on filigree
ornamentation.
Diameter - 240mm.
Burial mound, Archangelskaya
Sloboda village, Kakhovski area,
Khersonskaya district.
Excavated by A.M. Leskova, 1969.
MHTU, inv. No. AZS-2324.

*The lion motif on this torque often
appears on weaponry as the per-
sonification of strength and cunning. Torques originally were the
property of warriors but by 4th c.
BC they became part of women's
and children's attire.*

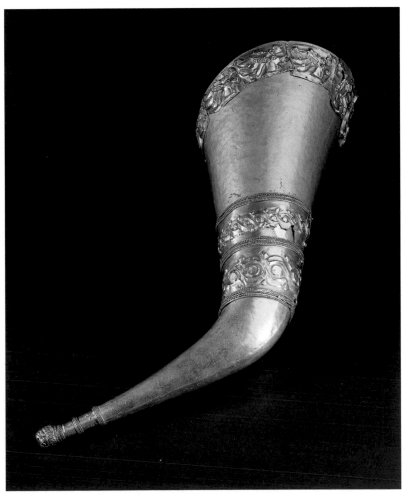

32

36. HEAD-DRESS WITH GOLD DECORATION

5th c. BC
Gold, fabric. Embossed.
Head-dress (reconstructed)-
Circumference of base - 560mm;
height - 160mm.
Burial mound, Bogdanovka village, Kakhovski area,
Khersonskaya district.
Excavated by A.I. Kubsheva,
1977.
MHTU, inv. No. AZS-3316-3318, NDF-205.

The head-dress may have been part of a wedding costume.

37. HEAD-DRESS WITH GOLD DECORATION.

4th c. BC
Gold, fabric. Embossed.
Head-dress (reconstructed)
Circumference of base - 560mm,
height - 160mm.
Burial mound, Volnaya Ukrayina
Krasni Perekopvillage, Kakhovski
area, Khersonskaya district.
Excavated by A.M. Leskov, 1970.
MHTU, inv. No. AZS-2410, 2416; NDF-206.

The decorative gold plates are original.

34. TORQUE

5th c. BC
Gold. Stamped, granulated,
drawn wire.
Length of torque - 460mm
Burial mound, Korneyevka village,
Veselovski area, Zaporozhskaya
district.
Excavated by V.V. Otroshenko,
1961.
MHTU, inv. No. AZS-3484.

This torque, made of braided gold wire with lion's head terminals probably came from workshops in the Greek colonies.

35. MIRROR

6th c. BC
Bronze. Cast.
Length - 310mm; diameter of the
disc - 175mm.
Chance find, Romenski area,
Sumskaya district.
NMHU, inv. No. B-1128.

Of Greek - Scythian style, this mirror may have been made in Olbia.

34

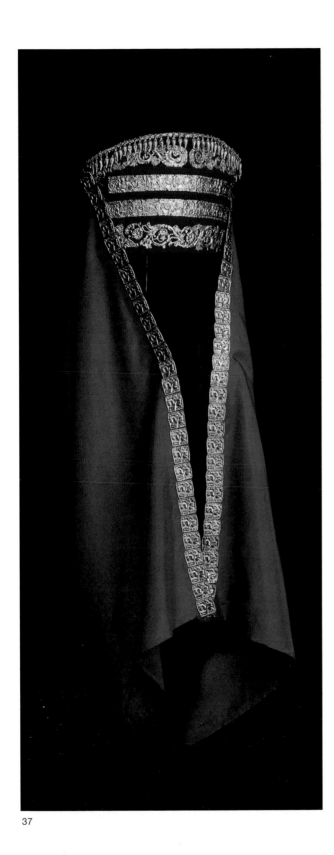

37

38. DECORATIVE PLATE FROM HEAD-DRESS

4th c. BC
Gold. Embossed.
Length - 365mm, breadth - 98mm.
Burial mound, Sachnovka village,
Morsun - Shevchenkovski area,
Cherkasskaya district.
Excavated by M. Geze, 1901.
MHTU, inv. No. DM-1639.

*The plate originally ornamented a
cylindrical head-dress similar to
that worn by the Scythian woman
depicted in the central image of
the composition. Made by a
Greek craftsman.*

39. PLAQUES FOR SEWING ON TO A GARMENT.

4th c. BC
Gold. Stamped.
each 19 x 20mm.
Burial mound Oguz , Nizhniye
Serogozi settlement,
Khersonskaya district.
Excavated by Y.V. Boltrika, 1980.
MHTU, inv. No. AZS-3454/1-60.

*The triangle was an ancient geo-
metric symbol embodying representations of the linking of three
elements - water, earth and air.*

40. NECKLACE

1st half of 5th c. BC
Gold. Punched, pressed, forged,
granulated, filigree.
Length - 475mm.
Burial mound, Volkovtsi village,
Romenski area, Sumskaya district.
Excavated by I.A. Linnichenko,
1898.
MHTU, inv. No. DM-6256/1-133.

41. TORQUE

4th c. BC
Gold. Cast.
Diameter - 175mm.
Burial mound, Volnaya Ukrayina
(Krasni Perekop) village,
Kachovski area, Khersonskaya
district.
Excavated by A.M. Leskova, 1970.
MHTU, inv. No. AZS-2411.

*Has terminals of recumbent
lionesses.*

38

42. BEADS FROM NECKLACE

4th c. BC
Paste.
Length - 540mm.
Burial mound, town of Melitopol,
Zaporozhskaya district.
Excavated by A.I. Terenozhnika,
1954.
NMHT, inv. No. B54-102.

*The necklace comprised 39 beads,
each decorated with stylized
depictions of an eye, a symbol of
protection.*

43. PENDANT IN THE SHAPE
OF A WOMAN'S HEAD

4th c. BC
Gold. Cast, granulated, filigree.
Height - 32mm; breadth -18.5mm.
Burial mound, Velikaya Belozerka
village, Kamensko - Dneprovski
area, Zaporozhskaya district.
Excavated by V.I. Bidzili, 1972.
MHTU, inv. No. AZS-2748.

*The head represented is that of a
female deity, perhaps Hera.*

44. PENDANT.

5th - 4th c. BC
Gold. Embossed, granulated, sol-
dered.
Height - 23mm; length - 19mm.
Location of find unknown.
MHTU, inv. No. DM-6327.

*Pendant in the form of a lion's
head with open jaws. The lion was
adopted as a motif by the
Scythians in the 5th century BC
due to the influence of Greek artistic traditions.*

45-46. DECORATIVE PLAQUES
IN THE FORM OF GRIFFINS (for
stitching to Garments).

End of 7th - beginning of 6th c.BC
Gold. Stamped.
29 x 26.5mm; 28.5 x 28mm.
Burial mound Perepyatikh,
Maryanovka village, Peryaslav -
Khmelnitski area, Kievskaya dis-
trict.
Excavated by M.D. Ivanishev,
1846.
MHTU, inv. No. AZS-984/5,8.

47. DECORATIVE PLAQUE (for
stitching to garment)

Second half of 4th c. BC
Gold. Stamped.
40.5 x 35.5mm.
Burial mound, Volkovtsi village,
Romenski area, Sumskaya district.
Excavated by S.A. Mazaraki,
1897.
MHTU, inv. No. DM-1717

*The model of the image was the
goddess Demeter or Athena as
represented on "blyaxi" (medallions) of Greek workmanship.*

43

48. DECORATIVE PLAQUE (for stitching to garment)

Second half of 4th c. BC
Gold. Stamped.
35 x 44mm.
Burial mound, Volkovtsi village,
Romenski area, Sumskaya district.
Excavated by S.A. Mazaraki,
1897.
MHTU, inv. No. DM-1706/6.

49. DECORATIVE PLAQUES DEPICTING SCENES OF SCYTHIAN BROTHERHOOD.

4th c. BC
Gold. Stamped.
28 x 27mm.
Burial mound, Berdyanska village,
Zaporozhskaya district.
Excavated by N.N.
Cherednichenko, 1977-1978.
MHTU, inv. No. AZS-3076/1-5.

50-51 DECORATIVE PLAQUES (for stitching to garment).

4th c. BC
Gold. Repousé.
35 x 38mm.
Burial mound Nosaki, Balki village,
Vasilievski area, Zaporozhskaya
district.
Excavated by V.I. Bidzili, 1970.
MHTU, inv. No. AZS-2696/1-2.

40

42

52. DECORATIVE PLAQUES (for stitching to garment)

5th c. BC
Gold. Stamped.
30 x 18mm.
Burial mound, Arkhangelskaya
Sloboda village, Kakhovski area,
Khersonskaya district.
Excavated by A.M. Leskov, 1969.
MHTU, inv. No. AZS-2338/1-105

*Five hundred plaques of different
forms had been attached to the
ceremonial attire of the leading
Scythian warrior in whose tomb
these items were found.*

53. EARRINGS

4th c. BC
Gold. Forged, drawn wire, granu-
lated, stamped.
Height: 1. - 115mm; 2. - 114mm.
Burial mound, Volchanskoye vil-
lage, Akimovski area,
Zaporozhskaya district.
Excavated by A.I. Kubishev, 1980.
MHTU, inv. No. AZS-3641/1-2
(illus. p. 20)

54. EARRINGS

4th c. BC
Gold. Stamped, punched, forged,
drawn wire.
Height: 1. - 88mm; 2. - 86mm.
Burial mound, Maryanovka village,
Bashtanski area, Nikolaevskaya
district.
Excavated by O.G.
Shaposhnikova, 1986.
MHTU, inv. No. 3839/1-2.

*The snake-legged goddess
depicted here is linked with legends surrounding the origins of
the Scythians. She was suppos-
edly the mother of Scythes, the
forefather of all the Scythian rulers.*

55. EARRINGS

4th c. BC
Gold. Stamped, forged, drawn wire.
1. Height - 70mm; diameter of ring - 35mm.
2.Height - 62mm; diameter of ring - 29mm.
Burial mound, Kamenka village, Ochakovski area, Nikolaevskaya district.
Excavated by O.G. Shaposhnikova, 1978.
MHTU, inv. No. AZS-3235/1-2.

56. EARRINGS

4th c. BC
Gold. Stamped, punched detail, forged, drawn wire.
Height: 1. - 82mm; 2. - 80mm.
Burial mound, Velikaya Znamenka village, Kamensko - Dneprovski area, Zaporozhskaya district.
Excavated by V.V. Otroshenko, 1982.
MHTU inv. No. AZS-3661/1-2.

The central image on the earrings may be the goddess Cybele.

57. EARRING

4th c. BC
Gold, enamel. Cast, engraved, granulated, enamelled on filigree ornamentation.
Height - 47mm.
Three Brothers burial mound, Ogonki village, Leninski area, Krimskaya district.
Excavated by D.S. Kirilin, 1965.
MHTU, inv. No. AZS-2282/1.

In the form of the figure of a sphinx sitting on a pedestal, and decorated with blue and green enamel.

58. BRACELETS

4th c. BC
Bronze, gold, enamel, paste.
Cast, plated, embossed,
engraved, enamelled on filigree
ornamentation.
Diameter: 1. - 80mm; 2. - 75mm.
Three Brothers burial mound,
Ogonki village, Leninski area,
Krimskaya district.
Excavated by D.S. Kirilin, 1965.
MHTU, inv. No. AZS-2281/1-2.

*The bracelets were for wearing on
the arm and are spiral-shaped,
wrapping round twice. The ends
are embossed with an ornate
lion's head.*

59. RING

5th c. BC
Gold, silver. Cast, engraved,
granulated, filigree.
Height - 41.3mm.
Incidental find, Tagencha village,
Kanevski area, Cherkasskaya dis-
trict.
MHTU, inv. No. AZS-657.

*Few examples of this type of ring
have been discovered in the northern Black Sea area and they have
all originated from Greece.*

60. RING.

4th c. BC
Gold. Forged, stamped.
21 x 21.5mm; diameter - 20mm.
Burial mound, Volnaya Ukrayina
(Krasni Pereskop) village,
Kakhovski area, Khersonskaya
district.
Excavated by A.M. Leskov, 1970.
MHTU, inv. No. AZS-2413/4.

*Mostly found in women's graves,
this type of ring was widespread in
Scythia during 4th - 3rd centuries
BC.*

57

61. RING

4th c. BC
Gold. Cast.
27 x 24mm.
Burial mound, Volnaya Ukrayina
(Krasni Perekop) village,
Kakhovski area, Khersonskaya
district.
Excavated by A.M. Leskov,
1970.
MHTU, inv. No. AZS-2414.

63. RING

4th c. BC
Gold. Embossed, filigree, soldered, inlaid work.
Bezel - 19 x 14mm; diameter of band - 27 x 15.5mm.
Three Brothers burial mound, Ogonki village, Leninski area, Krimskaya district.
Excavated by D.S. Kirilin, 1965.
MHTU, inv. No. AZS-2272.

The scarab-beetle was a popular amulet in ancient Egypt.

62. RING

4th c. BC
Gold. Cast, forged, engraved, granulated, filigree.
Bezel - 26 x 20mm; band - 33 x 24mm.
Burial mound Denisova Mogila, Ordzhonikidze village, Dnepropetrovskaya district.
Excavated by B.N. Mozolevskii, 1972 - 1975.
MHTU, inv. No. AZS-2956.

One of a small group of rings from the 4th century BC which are gold imitations of gemstone seals.

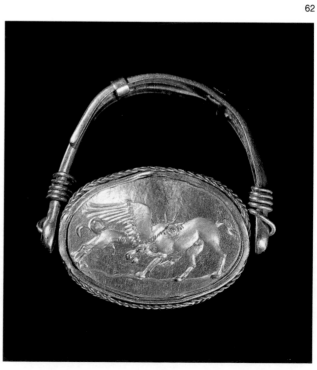

64. PECTORAL (replica)

Middle of 4th c. BC
Gold, enamel. Cast, forged, granulated, filigree.
Diameter - 306mm.
Burial mound Tolstaya Mogila,
town of Ordzhonikidze,
Dnepropetrovskaya district.
Excavated by B.N. Mozolevskii,
1971.
MHTU, inv. No. NDF-4.

*This highly ornate pectoral clearly
had religious significance, and its
imagery carries meanings which
were important to the Scythians.
These are once again closely
linked with images depicting life
(the upper layer) and those which
illustrated death (the lower layer).
The precise interpretation remains
unclear.*

64. Pectoral (detail)

65

66. FIBULA

Second half of 1st c. BC
Gold, bronze, rock crystal.
Embossed, cast, engraved, filigree.
Length - 78mm.
Nogaichinski burial mound,
Chervonoye village, Razdolnenski
area, Krimskaya district.
Excavated by A.A. Shchepinski,
1974.
MHTU, inv. No. AZS-2878.

*In the shape of a dolphin with a
body made from a single piece of
polished rock crystal and the head,
fins and tail made of gold.
Dolphins were a universal symbol
of love in ancient times.*

65. TORQUE

Second half of 1st c. BC
Gold, glass. Forged, cast,
engraved, blue glass inlay.
Diameter - 140mm.
Nogaichinksi burial mound,
Chervonoye village, Razdolnenski
area, Krimskaya district.
Excavated by A.A. Shchepinski,
1974.
MHTU, inv. No. AZS-2853.

*Although of striking appearance it
is coarsely made and the figures
are not well finished. It would
have been difficult to wear and
may have been made specially for
burial.*

66

SARMATIAN

67. FIBULA

1st - 2nd c. AD.
Gold, Garnet, glass. Forged, soldered.
51 x 54mm.
Nogaichinski burial mound, Chervonoye village, Razdolnenski area, Krimskaya district.
Excavated by A.A. Shchepinksi, 1974.
MHTU, inv. No. AZS-2864.

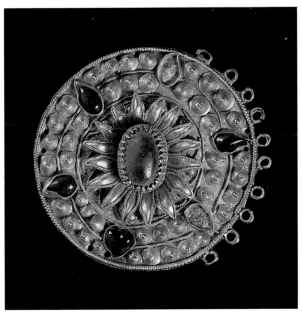

67

68. BRACELET

1st c. AD.
Gold, cornelian, glass. Forged, granulated, filigree, inlaid work.
Diameter - 65mm; breadth of band - 11mm.
Burial mound Sokolova Mogila Kovalevka village, Nikolaevski area, Nikolaevskaya district.
Excavated by G.T. Kovpanenko, 1974
MHTU, inv. No. AZS-3013/1.

68

GREEK CITY STATES

69. HYDRIA

5th c. BC
Bronze. Cast, forged.
Height - 440mm; diameter -
320mm.
Chance find, Peschanoye village,
Zolotonoshski area, Cherkasskaya
district, 1961.
NMHU, inv. No. B 41-433.

*A Greek vessel for holding water.
Part of a large set of bronze vessels (15) which are outstanding
examples of high art by Greek
craftsmen.*

70. SITULA

5th c. BC
Bronze. Cast, forged.
Height - 230mm; diameter -
155mm.
Chance find, Peschanoye village,
Zolotonoshski area, Cherkasskaya
district, 1961.
NMHU, inv. No. B41-437.

69

*Part of the same set of vessels as
Cat. No. 69. They provide evidence of trade links with Greece.*

71. RING

7th c. BC
Gold, Soapstone. Filigree, forged,
incised.
Bezel - 13 x 18mm; diameter of
band - 23mm.
Chance find, Western necropolis
Skifski Neapol.
MHTU, inv. No. AZS-1545.

*The soapstone scarab bears a
hieroglyphic inscription of the
Pharaoh Tuthmosis III (16th c. BC).
The ring was made much later,
probably in the 7th c. BC.*

72. PENDANT WITH GEM.

5th c. BC.
Gold, cornelian. Forged,
engraved, filigree, drawn wire.
Length of pendant - 22mm; bezel -
15 x 11mm.
Town of Kerch, Krimskaya district.
Date of find unknown.
From the collection of B.I. and V.N.
Khanenko.
MHTU, inv. No. DM-6093.

70 (detail)

73. RING WITH AN IMAGE OF HERMES.

5th c. BC
Gold. Cast, forged, engraved.
Diameter - 19mm.
Chance find in the vicinity of the town Kerch.
MHTU, inv. No. AZS-1692.

Hermes, the herald of the gods, is shown tying a sandal on his right foot. Rings of this type were widespread on the Black Sea Coast.

74. TORQUE

1st c. AD
Gold, cornelian. Forged, embossed, drawn wire.
Diameter - 164 x 170mm.
Panticapaeum. Modern town of Kerch, Krimskaya district.
Excavated by L.I. Chustova, 1953.
MHTU, inv. No. AZS-1719

Found in a child's grave. The cornelian bears an intaglio image of the young head of Apollo.

71

75. RING

2nd and 3rd c. AD
Gold. Cast, engraved.
Diameter - 23mm.
Tira. (Modern town of Belgorod-Dnestrovski), Odesskaya district.
Excavated by A.I. Furmanski, 1958.
MHTU, inv. No. AZS-1882.

74 (detail)

Ancient Coins

The Greek city states - the southern neighbours and permanent trading partners of the nomads - had their own coinage. So it is worth examining the minting of coins from gold, silver, and copper as one branch of toreutics (metal-working for artistic purposes). Given the extraordinarily high level of artistic culture among the ancient Greeks, it is not surprising to find that even such a purely utilitarian matter as coinage is treated as a branch of the applied arts. From the artistic point of view the coin is a unique form of miniature relief, and in genre and technology of production it is most closely related to intaglios, seals, and the small gold plaques which decorated most of the Scythian ceremonial clothes.

Tyras, Olbia, Chersonesus, and Panticapaeum (which in 480 BC became the capital of the powerful Bosporan state) all minted their own coinage. Imported coins have also been found in hoards from the south of the Ukraine, in particular the "kizikiny" which were coins made from electrum in the town of Kizik in the Sea of Marmara from the 6th to 4th centuries BC. For almost three centuries the kizikiny were a sort of inter-city-state currency, circulating in Asia Minor, Greece, and the northern Black Sea area, particularly in Olbia where they were the main means of settling large trade deals. They were displaced from this market only by the gold coins of Alexander the Great. In this exhibition there is a hoard found in the territory of ancient Olbia, which is now the village of Parutino in Nikolayev district.

The kizikiny from the hoard are dated to the 5th century BC. They are made from electrum, an alloy of gold and silver, using a rather simple technique. A bean-like piece of metal was placed on an anvil-mould engraved with a design, and was put under pressure from above using a rod (furnished with pins) through which it received the blows of a hammer. Thus an image was impressed on only one side of such archaic coins, including the kizikiny, the other bearing the traces of the pins, the so-called *quadratum incusum*. An invariable feature of all the electrum coins from Kizik is the town's emblem, a tuna fish. On different issues of the coins there are also other images which sometimes have a particular relationship with the tuna.

Thus on three of the kizikiny in our collection an eagle, lion and griffin are tearing the tuna to pieces (cat.nos.80, 82, 84). On a fourth there is a goat's head above the tuna (cat.no.81), and on another a scene from an ancient Greek myth - Zeus in the form of a bull, having seized Europa, is carrying her off on his back (cat.no.83). There was also found in Olbia a gold stater from Lampsacus in Mysia, a so-called lampsacin bearing the image of a fantastic winged creature (cat.no.85).

The kizikiny and lampsaciny were imported coins used for settling large foreign trade deals. As early as the 6th century BC Olbia had set up its own currency with characteristic features. Unlike other centres whose coins were minted in gold and silver, in Olbia the main circulation was in a non-precious metal - copper and its alloys. Olbia was the only one of the Greek city states to mint massive bronze coins (weighing about 100 grams) by the method of casting. On one side of the coins issued in the 5th and 4th centuries BC is an image of the Gorgon, serving the function of an apotropaion (or protection against evil), while on the other is an eagle and dolphin (cat.no.77).

In the 3rd century BC the large cast coins were replaced by smaller ones bearing the image of the god of the river Borysthenes (Dnieper); these are called "borisfeny". The profile head of Borysthenes in the form of a bearded man is very expressive (cat.no.78).

Panticapaeum, on the site of which the present town of Kerch is built, began minting its own coins in the 6th century BC. Gold staters were issued at the end of the 4th century with on one side the head of a satyr, and on the other a lion-headed griffin with a javelin in its jaws and aligned along an ear of wheat. In antiquity one of these staters had been used to make a ring (cat.no.79), which was found during the excavation of a Scythian burial in Dnepropetrovsk district. Some experts regard the satyr's head on the Panticapaeum coins as representing the Thracian god of Nature's fertility. As is appropriate for deities of the second rank representing a primary force of nature, the satyr on the Panticapaeum stater has a coarse, misshapen face. The "portrait" of the satyr is interpreted realistically and with marvellous expressiveness. The lines of the face are rendered in great detail - the dishevelled beard, the tuft of hair sticking out above the forehead, the deep wrinkles on the forehead and temples, and the spherical growth on the bridge of the nose which itself is snubbed. The satyr's head is decorated with an ivy wreath which suggests he belonged to the cult of Dionysus, who was the satyr's protector, the god of vegetation and fertility, and the patron of vine-growers and wine-makers. On a Panticapaeum obol of the 1st century BC Dionysus is represented in the form of a beautiful youth with soft, almost feminine features and an ivy wreath (cat.no.86).

A unique example of the coiner's art of the late Roman Empire is a gold medallion with a diameter of 55 mm (cat.no.76). In numismatics 'medallion' is the name given to coins struck for a commemorative or votive function, and which are greater - often very much greater - in weight than ordinary coins. In the Roman Empire gold medallions are known from the time of Augustus. They were issued on the occasion of this or that momentous event and were intended to be awarded as a mark of imperial favour. In part they were presented to military and civil dignitaries, but the largest ones of all were intended to appease barbarian chieftains whose tribes abutted the north-eastern borders of the empire. On neighbouring territories, and in particular in the Ukraine, gold medallions have turned up most probably as a result of trade.

The medallion referred to above is the largest Roman gold medallion found so far in the Ukraine. The image on the reverse side is directly related to the theme of nomadism. It was coined by Emperor Constantius II in honour of the victory of the Roman army in 358 AD over rebellious Sarmatian tribes, who inhabited the middle and lower Danube area in the 1st to 4th centuries. On the medallion we can see the victorious emperor in armour. In his right hand he holds a vanquished Sarmatian by the hair, with his hands tied behind his back. Above and to the right the emperor's head is being crowned by the goddess of victory, Victoria. The Sarmatian prisoner is portrayed realistically with clearly depicted face, clothes, and hairstyle. He is dressed in the characteristic Scythian and Sarmatian fashion in a jacket and pleated trousers. Representations of Sarmatians are rarely encountered in archaeological remains of this period, and the medallion's value lies in the unique opportunity it gives us to see what a 4th century AD nomad really looked like.

76. MEDALLION OF CONSTANTIUS II.

358 AD
Roman empire, Aquileia.
Gold.
Diameter - 55mm.
Verkhinivya village, Zhitomirskaya
district, 1976.
MHTU, inv. AU-1345.

Obverse: DN COVSTANTIVS
Bust of Emperor. facing right.
Reverse: VICTORIA AVGVS...T...
Emperor leading a vanquished
Sarmatian by his hair. In his left
hand the Emperor holds a
"labarum" with an image of Christ.

77. COIN

438-410 BC, Olbia
Bronze.
Diameter- 68mm.
Place of find unknown.
MHTU, inv. No. AE-2309.

Obverse: Head of Gorgon.
Reverse: APIX. Eagle on dolphin,
facing right.

78. BORISFEN

300-280 BC, Olbia
Copper
Diameter - 21mm.
Place of find unknown.
MHTU, inv. No. AE- 2322.

Obverse: Head of Borysthenes.
Reverse: OLBIO. Gorytus and axe.

79. RING MADE OUT OF A STATER

310-304 BC
Panticapaeum.
Gold.
Diameter - 19mm.
Verkhnaya Tarasovka village,
Dnepropetrovskaya district.
Excavated by N.N.
Cherednichenko, 1975.
MHTU, inv. No. AZS-3100.

Obverse: Head of bearded Satyr,
facing left.
Reverse: PAN. Griffin with a spear
in its jaws, facing left.

80. STATER-KISIKIN

5th c. BC
Kisik, Mysia.
Electrum.
Diameter - 21mm.
Parutino village, Nikolaevskaya
district.
MHTU, inv. No. AU-1172.

Obverse: Eagle, tearing a tuna fish,
facing left.
Reverse: Four indented squares.

81. STATER-KISIKIN

5th c. BC
Kisik, Mysia.
Electrum.
Diameter - 21mm.
Parutino village, Nikolaevskaya
district.
MHTU, inv. No. AU-1173.

Obverse: Head of a goat, facing
left. Below - a tuna fish.
Reverse: Four indented squares.

82. STATER-KISIKIN.

5th c. BC
Kisik, Mysia.
Electrum.
Diameter - 19mm.
Parutino village, Nikolaevskaya
district.
MHTU, inv. No. AU-1175.

Obverse: Griffin on a tuna fish, fac-
ing left.
Reverse: Four indented squares.

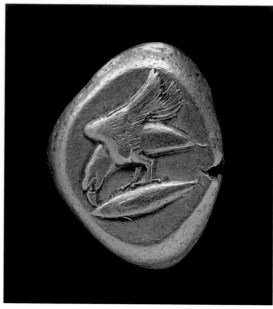

80

79

83. STATER-KISIKIN.

5th c. BC
Kisik, Mysia.
Electrum.
Diameter - 19mm.
Parutino village, Nikolaevskaya
district.
MHTU, inv. No. AU-1176.

*Obverse: Europa on a bull, facing
left. Below - a tuna fish.*
Reverse: Four indented squares.

84. STATER-KISIKIN.

5th c. BC
Kisik, Mysia.
Electrum.
Diameter - 19mm.
Parutino village, Nikolaevskaya
district.
MHTU, inv. No. AU-1177.

*Obverse: Lion on a tuna fish, fac-
ing left.*
Reverse: Four indented squares.

76

85. STATER-LAMPSACIN

5th c. BC
Lampsacus, Mysia.
Electrum.
Diameter - 20mm.
Parutino village, Nikolaevskaya
district.
MHTU, inv. No. AU-1394.

Obverse: Pegasus, facing left.
Reverse: Indented squares.

86. OBOL

80-70 BC
Bosporan kingdom.
Copper.
Diameter - 23mm.
Place of find unknown.
MHTU, inv. No. AE-2405.

*Obverse: Head of Dionysus wear-
ing a wreath, facing right.*
Reverse: Gorytus.

83

Jewelry from the fourth to fourteenth centuries: Nomads, Ancient Slavs, Kievan Rus

One of the characteristic features of our present age is a heightened interest in jewelry. And this is no accident. In the most free and direct manner jewelry has always reflected people's fundamental ideas about beauty in an aesthetic and even ethical expression of the most important rules and norms of life. Using the best examples of the museum's jewelry collection this chapter of the exhibition catalogue will introduce the reader to a short political history of the Ukraine from the 4th to 14th centuries AD, and to the characteristics of its jewelry.

The collection includes beautiful examples of the jeweller's art made from gold and silver using the most sophisticated methods of decorative metalwork. The techniques used include decorative filigree, engraved and chased ornament, niello work and gilding, coloured partitioned (cloisonné) enamelwork, and incrustation with semi-precious stones. The articles adorned ceremonial costume, weaponry, and horse harnesses; they were used both in religious, ceremonial and in everyday life. They have been found by archaeologists in excavations, not only as grave goods of the nomads but also in hoards left by the ancient slavs and Russians. Made by master jewellers from various tribes and peoples, the jewelry in the exhibition comes from an enormous steppe territory extending from the Volga to the Danube, and also from the forest-steppe and forest zones of the Ukraine.

From ancient times these regions have been settled by people differing from each other in ethnic origin, language, and material and cultural stages of development. The forest-steppe and forest zones were inhabited by agricultural tribes of ancient Slavs. In the southern Ukrainian steppe there lived many different tribes of nomadic herdsmen. There was a parallel historical development of the nomadic and agricultural peoples. Analysis of the relations between them shows that they were very complex, and as a rule developed in two directions - peaceful and military. Thanks to the permanent contacts between these two worlds, there was a steady interaction of the two cultures in various aspects of life - social, economic and political. It should also be said that a profound influence on both the nomads and the eastern Slavs was exercised by their relations with the Eastern Roman Empire, Byzantium.

Stormy events taking place in East Europe from the time of the great migrations to the invasion by the armies of Genghis Khan and Batu had a great effect on the course of history throughout Europe. These events may provisionally be divided into two phases. The first involved the invasion by the Huns into the European steppes, the fall of the Western Roman Empire, the appearance in Asia and Europe of the khanates (states of the nomadic and semi-nomadic type - Turkish, Avar and Khazar), the spread of ancient Slavs into Central Europe and the Balkans and their interminable struggle with Byzantium, the emergence of the eastern Slavs onto the historical scene, their consolidation and formation of extensive tribal alliances, one of which became the forerunner of the first eastern Slav state. These developments took place during the 4th - 8th centuries.

The second phase covered the 9th - 14th centuries. It was associated with the foundation and growth of the first ancient Russian state, Kievan Rus, and with the appearance in the area of the northern Black Sea steppes of the nomadic Pechenegs, the weakening and disappearance of the Khazar khanate, the supremacy over the steppes of the Polovtsy, and the Mongol invasion with the subsequent setting up of a state by the Golden Horde.

THE SOUTHERN UKRAINIAN STEPPES, 4th - 14th CENTURIES

The Huns (4th - 5th centuries)

The history of the Huns stretches back into antiquity. It is indissolubly linked with the history of the powerful grouping of nomadic tribes which occupied lands now in northern China in the second half of the first millenium BC. They were known by the Chinese as the Hsiung-Nu.

The nomadic Hsiung-Nu repeatedly attacked the northern districts of ancient China. To protect themselves from these raids, the Chinese began to build the Great Wall along their northern frontiers in the late 4th century BC. By degrees the Chinese drove the steppe tribes northwards beyond the Gobi Desert and into the steppes of modern Mongolia. In this area by the 3rd century BC the powerful Hsiung-Nu Empire had been created. Included in it were tribes in southern Siberia, Zabaykal, Mongolia, and Manchuria.

By the end of the 1st century AD, following uninterrupted wars with China and also internal dissension, the empire of the Hsiung-Nu split into two parts, southern and northern. The former came under the rule of the Chinese emperors, while the northern Hsiung Nu left their territory in AD 93 and began the "Great Raid" into the West. They ruled in Central Asia for more than 200 years. During this time they clashed with local Iranian-speaking tribes, the Sakas, Massagetae, and Issidones, with ancient Turkish and Ugrian tribes, and other peoples.

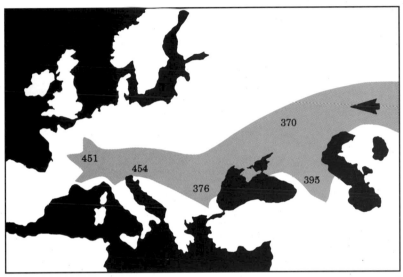

Hun spread

Some of them were exterminated or driven out, and others were assimilated. Thus the Hsiung-Nu, having originated in the Mongolian steppes, acquired a different set of ethnic and cultural characteristics. The main language of this conglomeration of tribes was a Turkish tongue.

In AD 375 an enormous mass of various Asian tribes, centred on the military power of the Hsiung-Nu, once more took up their drive westwards. In Europe they became known as the Huns. Crossing the Volga and Don, the Huns invaded the steppes of the northern Black Sea area. At this time the area was ruled over by two tribal alliances, the German Goths and the Iranian-speaking Sarmatians. After a ferocious battle with them the Huns emerged victorious. While assimilating some of the Goths and Sarmatians and building up their strength for a new campaign, the Huns remained in the East European steppes until 420. Then they crossed the Danube and advanced to the borders of Western Europe, plundering and laying waste everything en route. They laid siege to Constantinople in 434, but raised it when they were given a large ransom. Eventually they made the Central Danube steppes (Pannonia) their base.

In 445 Attila became leader of the Huns. His rule of the new nomad empire marked a period of great activity in Europe. It waged devastating wars with neighbouring countries, inspiring terror in their peoples. Provinces of the Western and Eastern Roman Empires were laid waste. The Huns raided right up to the banks of the Rhine, to Strasbourg and Orleans, and more than once threatened Constantinople. For its dependable rear the Hunnish Empire relied on the northern Black Sea area - nomadic tribes that had joined the Hun army and remained behind when the main force had left constituted an inexhaustible military reserve.

In 450 the Huns carried out a large incursion into Gaul. At Maurica in 451 (near Paris) there took place one of the greatest battles of antiquity. The Huns were opposed by an alliance of Romans, Gauls, and German tribes settled in Gaul within the Western Roman Empire. The battle was indecisive. However Attila ordered a retreat and they returned to Pannonia. In 454 the Hunnish Empire dissolved when Attila died.

The Hun invasion radically changed the southern part of Eastern Europe. As well as sparking off the "Great Migrations" of many European peoples, the steppe zone was occupied by Turkish-speaking tribes who killed off, drove out, or assimilated the former Iranian-speaking population of Scythians and Sarmatians.

The old centres of culture - the Greek colonies of the northern Black Sea area, which had now become Byzantine provinces - were almost entirely destroyed by the barbarians in the first years of Hun expansion. Other changes, no less far-reaching, occurred in the forest-steppe zone. The ancient Slav tribes were subjected to terrible ravages and were forced to move away into the forests to the north and north-east.

Evidence from archaeology and written sources show that, from the second half of the 4th century to the first half of the 5th, over the whole southern Ukrainian steppe a new culture arose among the nomads in the great migrations period. This was associated with the appearance of the Huns in the northern Black Sea area.

Among the steppe peoples of this region, the Hunnish polychrome style was widely disseminated in jewelry. Its chief features are the variety of colours, the form, design and ornamentation, and the decoration with semi-precious stones of a reddish hue. Hunnish ornaments were as a rule made from bronze and covered in gold leaf. They fall mostly into two main types. The first comprises objects with coloured semi precious stones in soldered groups, a background of gold, and filigree (cat.nos.87, 88, 89). In the second the artefacts have coloured semi-precious stones in soldered partitions, forming groups in various geometrical arrangements (cat.nos.90, 91). The exhibits show the Hunnish polychrome style very clearly.

Hunnish jewelry should not be viewed as the artistic products of one people, but rather exhibiting the influence of various cultures - ancient traditions, elements of Sarmatian and Gothic art, and new features brought in by the aggressive Huns. Experts believe that jewelry in the polychrome style was made in the Crimean province of Byzantium - the Bosphorus.

87

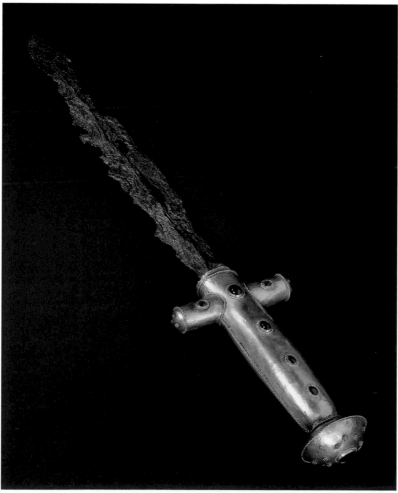

87. SWORD

4th - 5th c. AD
Gold, iron, garnet. Forged, granulated, filigree, inlaid work.
Length - 430mm.
Date and location of find unknown.
MHTU, inv. No. DM-1638.

The distinctive polychromatic style of its ornament indicates that it was made by the Huns. However, it was not used in war, since, firstly, the Huns carried swords with longer blades, and secondly, the decoration on the hilt would have made it uncomfortable to hold and use. It is likely that it was a ceremonial weapon. It is one of the best examples of jewellers' craftsmanship from the Hun era.

88. DECORATIVE MOUNT

4th - 5th c. AD.
Gold, cornelian. Embossed, granulated, inlaid work.
57 x 29mm.
Burial mound Kalinina state farm, Krasnogvardeiski area, Krimskaya district.
Excavated 1959.

MHTU, inv. No. AZS-1512.

Probably originally formed part of a diadem that was later cut into pieces, which were then sewn onto cloth as decoration.

89. BRIDLE MOUNT

4th - 5th c. AD
Gold, bronze, cornelian.
Embossed, soldered, inlaid work.
43 x 36mm.
Burial mound Kalinina state farm, Krasnogvardeiski area, Krimskaya district.
Excavated in 1959.
MHTU, inv. No. AZS-1519.

Overlay plate from a harness strap.

90. BELT BUCKLE

4th - 5th c. AD
Gold, cornelian. Cast, inlaid work.
40 x 26mm.
Chance find, Chikarenko village, Oktyaberski area, Krimskaya district.
Excavated in 1952.
MHTU, inv. No. AZS-1537.

The technique of partitioning the inlaid pieces is very rare, although the shape of the buckle is quite common.

91. STRAP-BUCKLE

4th - 5th c. AD
Gold, cornelian. Cast, inlaid work.
33 x 16mm.
Date and location of find unknown.
MHTU, inv. No. AZS-1904.

90, 91

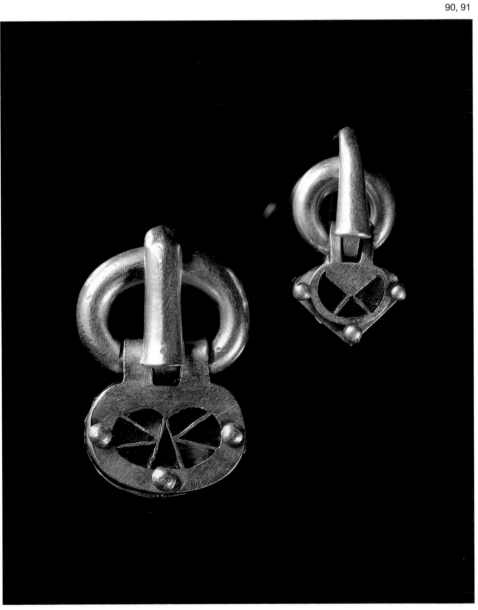

The Avars (6th - 7th centuries)

After the demise of the Hunnish Empire many nomadic tribes in the northern Black Sea area, no longer finding themselves under a central authority, quarrelled with each other and were unable to combine in a powerful tribal alliance to create a new empire on the steppes.

In the middle of the 6th century, Turkish-speaking tribes of nomads, called in Europe the Avars, crossed the Volga and Don from Central Asia and invaded the southern Ukrainian steppes. Some of the local tribes joined the Avar alliance as a result of which the Avars became much more numerous and powerful. During their occupation of the Black Sea area they waged constant war with local nomadic and ancient Slav tribes who had once more occupied their lands after the departure of the Huns into Western Europe. Some of these Slav tribes were forcibly incorporated into the Avar alliance.

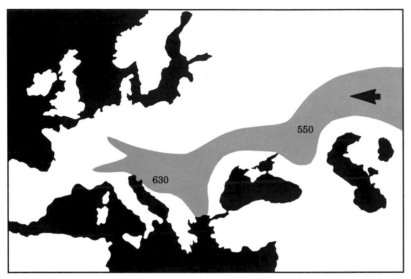

Avar spread

In 565 the united Avar forces crossed the Danube and invaded Byzantine territory; in 568 they became overlords of the Central Danube steppes. By the late 6th century a nomad military state made up of various tribes- the Avar Khanate- had arisen, at the core of which were the Avars. At its head was the khan Bayan. Contemporaries described him as a ruthless and skilful commander. The political history of the Avars in the Danube period recalls that of the Huns. It is a history of uninterrupted raids and military conflicts with the Franks and with Byzantium, and relentless plundering of the conquered peoples - the southern Slavs, Gepids and others. However in the mid 7th century the Avar Khanate crumbled under the impact of Frankish assaults and internecine dissension, and as a military and political force it ceased to exist.

During its existence a very distinctive culture had emerged. In the area of the northern Black Sea area steppes, archaeologists have found and studied a small but unique set of Avar cultural artefacts. This is to be explained by their short stay in the area, where they gathered their forces for a raid into the West. Other burials have been uncovered by archaeologists in the Central Danube area, and in these there have been found everyday objects, weaponry, and jewelry.

Avar weaponry is distinguished by a number of novel characteristics. As before, the main weapon of the nomads was the bow and arrow, although the Avar bows were considerably larger and longer-range. The spears too were longer and heavier. Replacing the straight, double-edged swords of the Sarmatians and Huns, there was introduced in the 6th - 7th centuries a longer, slightly curved, single-bladed sabre, intended for glancing blows. All these military innovations were possible thanks to the stirrup, which gave the rider more stability and accordingly a greater chance of success in hand-to-hand fighting on horseback. The development and introduction of new forms of weapon was one of the factors which gave the Avars rapid successes when they burst onto the historical scene.

Plates in the shape of shields are often encountered among the jewelry found in Avar burials in the northern Black Sea area and especially on the Central Danube. They consist of cast plaques for decorating leather belts. These belts, which came into fashion among the steppe peoples in the 6th - 7th centuries, served as a sign of social status, prosperity and military service (fig.1).

Most of the belt plates consist of bronze plaques with a smooth surface. There is decoration on a small number of them, which are made of silver, with simple geometrical or plant-based engraving. And in very isolated finds there are belt decorations that belong to the highest forms of jewelry.

There are two Avar examples in the exhibition (cat.nos.92, 93). These unique moulded silver plaques are skilfully decorated with partitioned inlay and fine niello. Judging by the rich ornamentation, the belt must have belonged to a member of the higher nobility. It is worth noting that analogous types of belt with modified and less sumptuous decoration are found even today among several of the peoples of the northern Caucasus and Central Asia.

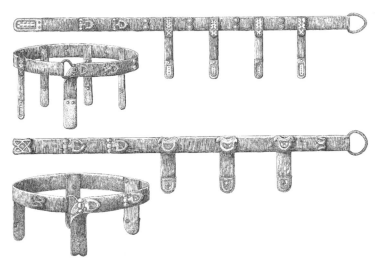

fig. 1 Reconstruction of belt fittings from the Avar period.

92. DECORATIVE PLAQUES FOR A BELT

5th - 7th c. AD
Gold, copper, silver, garnet.
Embossed, cast, granulated, inlaid work.
Burial mound Vasilyevska village, Khersonskaya district.
Excavated by A.I. Kubishev, 1984.
MHTU, inv. No. AZS-3648/1-19.

Made by Byzantine craftsmen, these highly coloured plaques have been uncovered in Avar graves over a wide area.

93. DECORATIVE PLAQUES FOR A BELT

6th - 7th c. AD
Gold, silver, bronze, garnet, glass.
Cast, embossed, granulated, inlaid work.
Burial mound, Razdolonoye settlement, Krimskaya district.
Excavated in 1966.
MHTU, inv. No. AZS-2831-2840.

92

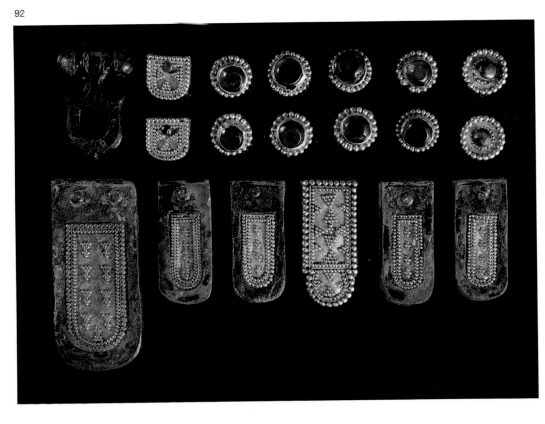

Khazars (7th - 8th centuries)

In the 7th - 8th centuries the northern Black Sea area steppes became part of one of the most powerful European states of the time - the Khazar Khanate. Its capital was Itil on the Lower Volga. The khanate was of the semi-nomadic type and comprised many tribes practising animal breeding, trade, and manufacture. The dominant tribe was the Turkish-speaking Khazars. Military raids, the seizure of new lands, and political alliances with Byzantium played an important part in establishing the political and economic strength of the khanate.

In 680 an extended war began with the Arabs, over supremacy in Transcaucasia. A powerful onslaught on Transcaucasia was called for not only in the Khazars' own interests, but also at the instigation of Byzantium, which was faced by a mortal threat from the Arabs in Asia Minor. In the end, the Khazars were victorious in this ferocious war. If it had not turned out thus, the subsequent history of Eastern Europe might have been very different. The spread of Islam, and with it eastern civilisation, was held up for several centuries at Europe's threshold in the Caucasus. The Khazars blocked the Arabs' way, just as the Franks under Charles Martel had done in the Pyrenees. In addition the Khazar Khanate, in the steppes between the southern Urals and the Caspian Sea, protected Europe from attack from the east by many nomadic Ugrian-Turkish tribes.

After consolidating their position in the Caucasus, by the mid-8th century the Khazar state had extended its power over the whole of the southern part of East Europe from the southern Urals to the Danube, over the Finno-Ugrian and Turkish peoples on the Volga, and also over territories to the north of the steppes which belonged to the ancient Slav tribes. This was a period in which the nomad state flourished both politically, economically, and culturally.

In the late 8th century, heathenism in the Khazar Khanate was exchanged for a new state religion - Judaism. It was accepted mainly by the upper strata in society - the khan and his circle. The chieftains of the individual tribes did not accept it, but remained heathen. As a result of religious dissension a civil war broke out that lasted for about a century. This led to a serious weakening of the khanate, which was exploited by Asian nomads - the Magyars and Pechenegs. At the end of the 9th century they invaded Khazar territory and gradually whittled away the Khazars' power. The last blow against the khanate was wielded by Kievan Rus in the second half of the 10th century, and it ceased to exist following military campaigns by the Kievan princes in 965 and 969.

Throughout the whole history of the Khazars, trade was an important part of their lives, exports and imports being of equal importantance. Customs duties collected from trade caravans crossing their territory and tribute from subject peoples also strengthened the state's economy. As mentioned earlier, the Byzantine Empire exerted a huge influence on all aspects of Khazar society. From the metropolis and its Black Sea provinces the Khazars received a variety of goods including a large amount of jewelry which they had commissioned.

The exhibition includes artefacts from two very rich burials dating from the heyday of the Khazar state. Among them a massive gold decoration to be worn on the chest stands out for its beauty and sophisticated execution (cat.no.98). In some of its details, rendered in the polychrome style, the traditions of earlier Byzantine jewelry can be traced. This is seen in stylistic features (the manner of decorating the surface with coloured insets of semi-precious stones, and filigree ornament of gold wire and spherules), and also in certain technical methods of placing the stone insets in soldered groups.

These two rich burials of Khazar khans were discovered by archaeologists on the boundary between the forest-steppe and the steppe. They apparently resulted from Khazar military assaults against Slav tribes. It was concluded from research into these burials that they involved cremation, which was characteristic of the 7th - 8th century nomadic peoples in the Eurasian steppe zone from the Altai foothills to the Danube.

94-95. TWO PSEUDO-BUCKLES

7th - 8th c. AD
Gold, tourmaline. Cast,
embossed, granulated, inlaid
work.
59 x 33mm; 61 x 33mm.
Kelegei treasure, Gladkovka village, Golopristanski area,
Khersonskaya district.
Excavated in 1927.
MHTU, inv. No. AZS-1432-1433.

*On the Steppes most of the population wore ordinary belts and
only those of high standing wore
belts with pseudo-buckles.*

96. EAR PENDANTS

7th - 8th c. AD.
Gold. Embossed, soldered, granulated.
Height - 74mm; 71mm.
Date and location of find
unknown.
MHTU, inv. No. AZS-1907/1-2.

*Used to decorate the head-
dresses of high ranking nobility.
They were made by Byzantine
craftsmen.*

97. PENDANT

7th - 8th c. AD
Gold. Embossed, granulated, soldered, inlaid work.
Height - 118mm.
Burial mound, Glodossi village,
Maloviskovski area,
Kirovogradskaya district.
Excavated by A.Y. Smilenko,
1961.
MHTU, inv. No. AZS-1957.

*Found in one of the richest graves
from the period. The site was discovered by chance in 1961 by a
school pupil, and then researched
by archaeologists.*

98. CHEST DECORATION

7th - 8th c. AD.
Gold. Embossed, soldered, granulated, filigree.
Length - 267mm.
Burial mound, Glodossi village,
Maloviskovski area
Kirovogradskaya district.
Excavated by A.T. Smilenko,
1961.
MHTU, inv. No. AZS-1967-1968

97

98

The Pechenegs and Polovtsy (10th - 13th centuries)

After the final collapse of the Khazar Khanate, the southern Ukrainian steppes came under the rule of the Pechenegs (10th - first half of 11th centuries), and then of the Polovtsy (mid 11th - first half of the 13th centuries). The Pecheneg armies first appeared in the northern Black Sea area steppes in the late 9th century. By the beginning of the 10th century they had completely taken over the territory between the Don and Danube. Their original homeland was the steppes of Central Asia north of the Aral Sea.

The whole period of Pecheneg supremacy was marked by their plundering raids on the Byzantine provinces in the Crimea (Bosphorus and Khersonesus), Bulgaria, Hungary, Kievan Rus, and the lands of the people living along the Don and Volga and in the northern Caucasus. In 1036 the united Pecheneg armies were routed by Rus forces near Kiev. After this defeat the main mass of nomads went west beyond the Danube. What remained of the Pechenegs partly went into the service of the Kievan princes, while others were annihilated by new nomadic invaders - the Polovtsy.

The Polovtsy stemmed from the steppes of northern Kazakhstan and southern Siberia. Having dealt with the rump of the Pechenegs, they acquired the dominant role in the East European steppes from the Volga to the Danube. For two centuries the Polovtsian armies carried out repeated raids into neighbouring territories. They frequently crossed the Danube and invaded Central Europe, ravaging the southern lands of Kievan Rus.

The ancient Rus state succeeded in repulsing the Polovtsian incursions. The Kievan princes directed the struggle against the Polovtsy which continued from the mid 11th to the mid 13th century, when the Polovtsian state was destroyed by the Mongols. Some of the Polovtsy joined the Mongols' tribal alliance.

Among the many barrows which fill the southern Ukrainian steppes, there is a distinct group of comparatively small burials from Pecheneg and Polovtsian times. Also a significant number of Pecheneg and Polovtsian graves were inserted into large barrows from earlier times (Bronze Age, Scythian, Sarmatian). The most widespread finds in the graves of these nomads are horse harnesses and a large amount of assorted weaponry.

The exhibition includes a very rare find from the grave of an aristocratic Pecheneg warlord - a set of bridle ornaments (cat.no.99). It consists of silver figured plaques which were decorations for the straps of a bridle (10th - first half of 11th century). The plaques were cast and ornamented with gilding and niello inlay. The source of the techniques for producing ornamentation in the form of plants and strapwork can be traced back to the eastern Mediterranean tradition, or more exactly to Byzantine art of the 9th - 11th centuries. Direct contacts between the nomads and the populations of the Byzantine provinces in the Crimea encouraged the dissemination of bridal decorations with basically Byzantine decoration among the Pechenegs of the northern Black Sea area.

Polovtsian objects of the greatest interest are exhibited from the Chingul barrow. They are a unique incense burner (cat.no.103) of West European manufacture, made with great skill and artistry, and a unique Ancient Rus iron war helmet (cat.no.102), decorated with thick gold plating and ornamentation along the lower edge.

99 BRIDLE ORNAMENTS.

10th - 11th c. AD
Silver. Cast, engraved, nielloed,
gilded.
Cross-shaped overlay - 40 x
40mm.
Tips - 55 x 22mm; 62 x 14mm.
Strap coverings - 80 x 55mm.
Diameter of round plates - 15mm.
Burial mound, Novo-Kamenko village, Kakhovski area,
Khersonskaya district.
Excavated by A.I. Kubishev, 1974.
MHTU, inv. No. AZS-3289/1-21.

*The decorative elements on these
straps did not play the same role
at this time as in previous periods.
It is clear that these were not
signs of merit, but were simply
decoration. However, the horse's
harness shows considerably richer
ornamentation than that of a common horse- owner. The piece was
made in workshops in the Crimea.*

100. SHIELD BOSS

13th c. AD, 1240 - 1260
Silver. Stamped, gilded.
Diameter - 187mm.
Chingul burial mound,
Zamozhnoye village,
Zaporozhskaya district.
Excavated by V.V. Otroshenko,
1981.
MHTU, inv. No. AZS-3624.

*From a site now accepted to have
been the burial place of a
Polovstian Chief. Defensive armour
is very rare in finds from nomads'
graves.*

101. ROD

12th - 13th c. AD
Gold. Forged.
Length - 420mm.
Chingul burial mound,
Zamozhnoye village,
Zaporozhskaya district.
Excavated by V.V. Otroshenko,
1981.
MHTU, inv. No. AZS-3608.

102. HELMET

12th - 13th c. AD
Iron. Cast, forged, gilded.
Diameter - 200mm; height -
230mm.
Chingul burial mound,
Zamozhnoye village,
Zaporozhskaya district.
Excavated by V.V. Otroshenko,
1981.
MHTU, inv. No. AZS-3607.

*Of ancient Russian origin. The
helmet illustrates the resemblance
between the attire of a Russian
prince and a Polovtsian ruler. It
underlines the fact that a small
Polovtsy horde served under the
leadership of the khan Tichak in
the host of Danil Galitski.*

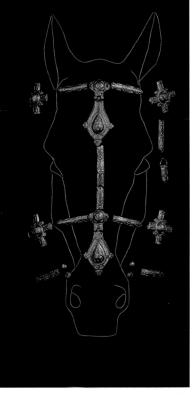

99

103. INCENSE-BURNER

12th - 13th c. AD
Silver. Cast, forged, engraved,
gilded.
Height - 310mm.
Maximum diameter of the bowl
and cover - 165mm.
Chingul burial mound,
Zamozhnoye village,
Zaporozhskaya district.
Excavated by V.V. Otroshenko,
1981.
MHTU, inv. No. AZS-3623.

*Similar vessels were made by
French and German craftsmen in
the 12th-13th centuries. The
incense-burner was probably filled
with flowers, leaves and stems,
which were used for making
smoke for medicinal purposes or
as part of religious rites.*

100-103

The Mongols and the Golden Horde (13th - 14th centuries)

In the early 13th century, a very powerful Mongol nomad state was founded in Central Asia under Genghis Khan. One of the chief constituent tribes was the Mongols, also known as the Tatars. Beginning in 1206, the Mongol armies seized northern China, Manchuria, and territories in south-eastern Siberia, Central and south-western Asia, and East Europe. By 1242 nomad armies, under the command of khan Batu (grandson of Genghis Khan), after devastating and subjugating many Asian and European states, reached the borders of North Italy and Germany. Such a threat from steppe nomads had not faced Europe since the invasion of the Huns. However in late 1242, at the most critical moment for Western Europe, khan Batu turned his armies about and headed east to the Volga steppes.

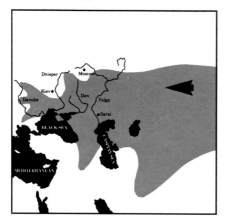

As a result of aggressive campaigns, three western branches of the empire founded by Genghis Khan emerged. For a while they were dependent on the great khan of the Mongols in their capital Karakorum in Mongolia, but later they became independent states. The largest of the three was the domain of Jochi, the eldest son of Genghis Khan, and it included West Siberia, the Priural and Volga region, the northern Caucasus, the Crimea, northern Khorezm, and the lands of the Polovtsy and other tribes and peoples living on the vast steppes from the Irtysh to the Danube. Jochi's domain, named subsequently the Golden Horde, was founded by khan Batu in 1243. Its capital was the town of Sarai on the Lower Volga. The ancient Slav state did not join the Golden Horde, although it was largely dependent on it, and paid an annual tribute to the Mongol khans.

The Golden Horde was one of the most powerful states of Eurasia in the 13th and the first half of the 14th centuries. It lasted more than 200 years, eventually disintegrating into separate states - the Kazan, Astrakhan, Siberian and Crimean Khanates - as a result of internecine conflict and the growing power of the princes in Moscow.

The cultural characteristics of this enormous multi-ethnic alliance were determined by the political, economic, and social peculiarities of life in the state. This was expressed in the interaction of the steppe nomads' culture with the syncretic culture of the towns which were populated not only by Mongols, but also by Polovtsy, Bulgars, Russians, Finno-Ugrian people from the Volga region and the Urals, immigrants from Western Europe and Central Asia, Iran, the Crimea, the Caucasus, China, India, and so on. They were responsible for creating the urban culture, at the core of which appeared the traditions and artistic characteristics of the settled and highly developed civilisations of the native peoples.

Jewelry held a prominent position among the various forms of manufacture of art objects. It expressed in full measure the tastes and ideologies of the steppe and urban elites. Vivid examples of Golden Horde jewelry may be seen in the exhibition. They are a silver goblet and a silver ladle (cat.nos.104,105). The main features common to these exhibits are the technique of ornamentation and the composition. The figures in the design are enclosed within a special band of ornamentation - in gilded medallions, rosettes and borders. The motifs are in the Golden Horde style, although the shape of the ladle's handle in the form of a dragon's head is Chinese, traceable to the 3rd - 4th centuries. Golden Horde jewelry also borrowed the lotus flower from Chinese art. The shape of the flowers are typical of the first quarter of the 14th century. There are not many vessels with dragon's head handles. So far only eight similar ladles have been found , seven in the Ukraine and Russia, and the eighth in China.

Having read the chapter on Scythian and Sarmatian art, the reader will know that most of the fine jewelry from the ancient world in the exhibition came from Greek workshops, mainly in the colonial cities of the northern Black Sea area. These Greek city states much later became provinces of the Eastern Roman Empire of Byzantium. Even at that time Byzantine craftsmen had regular contacts with the steppe peoples and were commissioned by representatives of the richer classes of various nomad communities to make expensive articles of jewelry.

Byzantine art preserved stable traditions from antiquity, but also absorbed various elements from the art of the ancient Far East. It was required to express and personify in its imagery the power and wealth of the empire. A prime example of Byzantine jewelry from the 12th century is a drinking cup which was discovered in Chernigov (cat.no.153). It is ornamented with engraved and chased patterns, niello and gilding. The outer sides of the embossed oval medallions are decorated with plant designs and mounted warriors - a Byzantine with a spear and a Polovtsian shooting an arrow. The bottom of the cup is decorated with an interesting scene depicting the Emperor, playing on a musical instrument, and a dancer, and around them birds and animals. Similar cups, though not quite so sumptuous, are encountered in small numbers in the late 11th and early 12th centuries in the Middle East, Iran, Afghanistan and Central Asia.

104. GOBLET

End of 13th - 14th c. AD.
Silver. Forged, engraved, gilded.
Height - 140mm; diameter of bowl
- 100mm; base - 72mm.
Kiev. Date of discovery unknown.
MHTU, inv. No. AZS -865.

The ornamentation on this work stems from Chinese traditions and motifs. It is characteristic of the Golden Horde period in the 13th - 14th centuries.

106

104

105. "KOVSH" (LADLE)

End of 13th c. /beginning of 14th c. AD
Silver. Forged, engraved, gilded.
Height with handle - 60mm; diameter - 130mm.
Kiev. Date of find unknown.
MHTU, inv. No. AZS-863.

The handle is shaped in the form of a dragon's head. The prototype for this work was Chinese, but the working of the initial material shows Asian influence.

106. DEFENCE OF KIEV AGAINST THE MONGOL-TATARS.

by V. Shatalin, 1952.
Watercolour on board.
430 x 365mm.
MHTU, inv. No.M-1365.

The picture depicts the capture of Kiev by Mongol hordes under the leadership of khan Batu on the 6th of December, 1240. The painting shows the final moments of the defence of the town on the citadel near the Desyatina Church. In the centre is the figure of the voivode Dmitri, heading the defence of Kiev.

The ancient East Slavs (6th - 8th centuries)

In European history the second half of the first millenium was a period of great disruptions. The migrations of many peoples and their struggle with the Roman Empire on its western borders came to an end, while in the east, on the borders of the Byzantine Empire, they continued into the 6th and 7th centuries. This period was very important for the history of the Slavs, and their significance on the European political stage rapidly increased.

The beginning of their history is lost in the mists of time. There is plentiful evidence to suggest that their original homeland was between the Middle Dnieper and the basin of the Vistula, and possibly also that of the Oder. Their economy was based on agriculture, and from it sprang animal breeding. Hunting, fishing and bee keeping also played an important role, since the natural conditions were favourable for them.

Together with other tribes they carried on a prolonged struggle with the Byzantine Empire during the 6th - 7th centuries. This period has become known as the Balkan Wars. Numerous raids by the Slavs over the imperial borders were accompanied by the migration of a considerable proportion of the Slav people to the Balkan Peninsula, which they almost entirely took over. These tribes moved from their homeland not only south-westwards in the direction of the Danube and Balkans, but also westwards, reaching the Elbe, and northwards to the Gulf of Finland and eastwards to the Upper Volga. This widespread migration led to the separation of the East, West and South Slavs, which was essentially completed in the second half of the first millenium.

The East Slavs settled in territory bordering the Carpathians in the west, the Gulf of Finland in the north, the Upper Volga in the east, and the northern Black Sea steppes in the south, the latter occupied by nomads. During the Slav migrations, a large alliance of tribes emerged in East Europe which subsequently took the form of a military and political state. The Middle Dnieper region played an important role in the history of the East Slavs; it was occupied by Poles and was to become the nucleus of the future ancient Russian state, Kievan Rus. The Poles were the most powerful element in the tribal alliance, which neighbouring tribes also joined. Located on the edge of the forest-steppe, this alliance played a very important role in the life of all the Slav tribes along the Dnieper. For one thing, in a fierce struggle, it withstood the onslaught of the steppe nomads - Avars, Bulgars, Khazars, and others - and this helped to create the conditions for an intensive development of the economy, culture and art.

As a result of the development of manufacture and trade among the Eastern Slavs, in particular in the Middle Dnieper region in the 6th - 8th centuries, towns arose which functioned as manufacturing, trading and tribal centres. One of these settlements became the capital of the Polish tribal alliance and the centre of Rus. Thus were laid the foundations of Kiev.

In the trading and manufacturing settlements, there was rapid development of metal-working, smithery and jewelry. One of these was the village of Kharevka, where a large quantity of jewelry made by East Slav craftsmen has been found in hoards. The main methods of working metal artistically were surface and bulk casting, and forging. Minting, punching, and stamping on moulds were also techniques used. Some artefacts were decorated with filigree, niello and pseudo-niello. Some of the most widely distributed ornaments at that time were ear pendants and fibulae (brooches) with finger-like projections (cat. nos. 109, 110, 111).

Magnificent objects were made from precious metals. They reveal not only the tastes of all sections of society but also their religious beliefs. Outstanding examples of 6th century craftsmanship were found in the Martynov hoard. They include small figurines of men and horses (cat.nos.107, 108). These were cast in silver using the *cire perdue* method, and partly gilded. The pieces from 6th - 8th century hoards demonstrate the advanced development of jewelry among the East Slavs which was fundamental to the decorative applied arts of Kievan Rus.

107. PLAQUE

6th - 7th c. AD
Silver. Cast, engraved, gilded.
Length - 96mm; breadth - 62mm.
MHTU, inv. No.AZS-82.

Ornamentation for clothing or horses' harness. In Europe in the 6th -7th centuries only isolated zoomorphic and anthropomorphic pieces like these were known.

Along with the following two exhibits this comes from the Martinovsk Treasure, discovered at Martinovka village in Cherkasskaya district. The find was made in 1907, but all of the 120 pieces were not recovered at that time. Indeed, some later found their way to the British Museum. They are probably all trophies taken in battle.

108. PLAQUE

6th - 7th c. AD
Silver. Cast, engraved, gilded.
Length - 76mm.
MHTU, inv. No. AZS-86.

109. DIGITATE FIBULA

6th - 7th c. AD
Silver. Cast, engraved, gilded.
Height - 170mm; breadth -
81.5mm.
MHTU, inv. No. AZS-36.

Widely used among the Antai people and it is considered that they were important symbols for this Slavonic group.

110-111. EAR PENDANTS

7th - 8th c. AD
Silver. Gilded, granulated, cast, forged.
Height - 60mm; 57mm; 59mm.
Burial mound Kharyevka village, Putivilski area, Sumskaya district.
Chance find, 1949.
MHTU, inv. No. AZS-2179, 2180/1-2.

The forms of these pieces reflect the beliefs of the Eastern Slavs. These are linked to the ancient Slavonic cult of the earth, fertility, marriage and the family.

Kievan Rus (9th - 13th centuries)

As already mentioned, from the 7th to the first half of the 9th centuries large tribal alliances were set up in the eastern Slav lands. They reflect the process of forming a state among the East Slavs. At this time new circumstances arose, including the advanced development of the economy, in particular agriculture and manufacture, which accelerated the collapse of earlier tribal relations. Various trading links with the Arabian East and Byzantium, the necessity of defending their land from raids by steppe nomads, and the general improvement of the economy brought about favourable conditions in the last quarter of the 9th century for the setting up of a common eastern Slav state. The unification of the northern (based on Novgorod) and southern (Kievan) lands, which occurred under Prince Oleg (882 - 911) completed the formation of the first ancient Russian state, Kievan Rus. Its capital was Kiev, which had been founded in the late 5th or early 6th century.

Kievan Rus, which during the 10th century united all the eastern Slav tribes, became one of the most powerful European states of the time. The culmination of its historical development was reached during the reign of Prince Vladimir Sviatoslavich (978 - 1015). He was one of the most talented rulers of his period. He devoted all his energies to the unification and consolidation of the state. In 988 Prince Vladimir accepted Christianity which in time became the state religion. In ousting pagan beliefs, Christianity assisted in the extension and strengthening of political, economic and cultural relations with other countries in Europe and the East, and in the stabilisation of relations between its own lands. Also, the new religion furthered the extensive penetration into Rus of the influence of the advanced Byzantine culture, which in turn encouraged the development of the literature, architecture and art already existing in the country.

After Vladimir's death, the Kievan throne was occupied by his son Yaroslav, known amongst the people as "The Wise". This great prince (1019 - 1054) continued his father's policies. His rule was marked by a further improvement in the fortunes of Rus and its capital. At the same time the state was expanding towards the Baltic and the Carpathians. Yaroslav had Kiev surrounded by strong defences. Monumental buildings were erected within the city: churches, cathedrals and palaces, and it became a great political, economic and cultural centre in East Europe. Foreign merchants and travellers compared Kiev in its beauty and opulence to the capital of Byzantium, Constantinople.

Kievan Rus maintained friendly relations with many other countries - Byzantium, Germany, France, Hungary, Poland, Scandinavia, the Khazar Khanate, the Volga Bulgars, and so on. During the rule of Yaroslav the Wise, the threat arose of invasion by the Pechenegs from the steppe. In 1036 they were finally beaten in a battle near Kiev.

At the end of the 11th century Yaroslav's grandson, Prince Vladimir Monomakh, entered the political arena. During his reign he attempted to preserve the political unity of all the lands of Ancient Rus. He also organised, with other princes, successful raids against the steppe armies of the Polovtsy whose attacks were increasing. By that time the prestige of Kievan Rus on the international scene had grown enormously. Relations with neighbouring states were particularly strengthened. The original and distinctive culture of Kievan Rus had an outstanding influence on the development of world culture. Its great achievements included architecture, painting, literature, and the decorative applied arts, one of these being jewelry.

Jewelry often contains valuable information concerning not only the development of manufacturing techniques, but also the cultural relations, mutual influences, traditions, and tastes of all sections of society. In hardly any country of the medieval world can one find evidence of such a cultural melting-pot as in Rus, which lay at the crossroads of trade routes between Scandinavia and Byzantium. Imported artefacts, primarily of Byzantine manufacture, were not only in demand by the richer strata of society but also served as models for the creations of the ancient Rus master jewellers. However, as in earlier times, Kievan Rus superimposed its own national character on the designs and ornamentation in accordance with local traditions and customs.

In the development of jewelry in Rus, the Kievan craftsmen played a significant part. Analysis shows that the finest masterpieces were made in Kiev, the centre of jewelry manufacture in the old Rus state. The Kievan jewellers used all the various techniques which were known in the most advanced countries - niello, filigree, casting, minting, forging, engraving, stamping, punching, incrustation, inlay on gold and silver, and also a technique borrowed from Byzantium and a miracle of ancient jewelry - cloisonne´ enamelwork (coloured enamel separated by fine metal walls).

The magnificent works of Old Rus art emerging from the Kievan workshops enjoyed a wide demand, not only within Rus but also abroad. The fame of the Kievan craftsmen was so great that as late as the 12th century the monk Theophilus Presbyter, of Paderborn Monastery, praised them in his tract on the jeweller's art. He placed the silver and gold smiths of Rus second only to those of Byzantium for the perfection of their enamel and inlay work.

Unique exhibits from the 11th - 13th centuries in the museum collection are distinguished by unusual form and exquisite execution. Among decorations for Ancient Rus princely and boyar dress of the 11th - 13th centuries, the heyday of jewelry in Kievan Rus, there are gold and silver kolti(head-dress pendants) with ryasni(chains), silver nielloed bracelets worn on the arm and twisted bracelets with hammered out terminals, silver twisted and plaited chains for the chest and necklaces, three-beaded earring pendants, massive gold torques, and a great many other ornaments which even now delight the eye with the purity of their colours, perfection of form, and decoration (cat.nos.125-127, 134-150, 154-160) (fig.1, 2).

A set of unique coins deserve a special place in the collection. These were in circulation in Kievan Rus during the 9th - 13th centuries. It should be mentioned that the first coins in Eastern Europe appeared in the 8th century. From then on the Slav people used large quantities of Arabic silver dirhems (cat.nos. 112, 113). They fulfilled the basic functions of currency, and were minted in the large territory of the Arabian Khanate. Through more than two centuries, the dirhems turned up in the East Slav principalities, and then in Rus, arriving by two main routes - a southern one via the Khazars, and a northern one via the Volga Bulgars. The most active importation was in the mid-10th century, though by the end of the century it had virtually ceased.

The first Rus coins made their appearance in the late 10th or early 11th century (cat.nos.114, 115). The small number of ancient Rus coins found suggests that they were not minted for long. So far about 300 silver coins have been found. The Kievan coins of the 10th - 11th centuries are wonderful examples of the national culture. The issue of its own coins was a unique affirmation of the sovereignty of the Kievan state, enhanced by skilful minting and original declarative inscriptions. From the late 11th century the main unit of currency in Rus was the grivna. This was a silver ingot in use during the 12th - 14th centuries (cat.nos.128 - 133).

In conclusion it should be said that the development of Ancient Rus culture was cut short by the Mongol invasion. But the spiritual and cultural achievements of Kievan Rus did not die; they became that inexhaustible source which served as the foundation for the creative achievements of the Ukrainian, Russian and Belorussian peoples.

fig. 2 : Reconstruction of ceremonial head-dress of a woman from the royal household, 12th - 13th centuries.

fig. 1 : Reconstruction of the ceremonial dress of a prince, 12th - 13th centuries

112-113. "DIRHEM" (Silver coins)

9th - 10th c. AD
Silver. Minted.
Diameter - 26 x 23mm.
Location and date of find
unknown.
MHTU, inv. No. SR-717, 718.

*Unit of Arabian currency intro-
duced in the 7th century. With the
appearance of these dirhem in
Eastern Europe the circulation of
currency began to grow. Trade
expanded with minted money
instead of by the exchange of
goods.*
*Dirhem were widely used by
ancient Russian peoples until the
beginning of the 11th century.*

114-115. "SREBRENIK" (Silver coins)

11th c. AD
Silver. Cast, minted.
Diameter - 28mm; 32mm.
Treasure from the town of
Nezhina, Chernigovskaya district.
Chance find, 1852.
MHTU, inv. No. AU-725, 726.

*The Srebrenik was the first silver
coin of the people of Kiev Rus. It
was minted to underline the rise of
Kiev Rus. Srebenik were cast
instead of the normal process of
cutting from sheets of metal.*

116

116. SWORD

10th c. AD
Silver, iron. Forged, engraved,
nielloed.
Length of hilt - 170mm; length of
blade - 640mm.
Found in the city of Kiev,
Vladimirskaya street.
Excavated in 1901.
MHTU, inv. No. AZS-329.

*Made by Southern Russian crafts-
men, using Eastern motifs.
Discovered in the grave of a member of a prince's armed force.*

117. FIBULA

10th c. AD
Silver. Gilded, cast, forged.
Diameter of ring - 76mm; length of
rod - 240mm.
Found in the city of Kiev.
Chance find, 1900.
MHTU, inv. No. AZS-339.

*Of a ring-shaped Scandinavian
type.*

121

118-120. LEAF-SHAPED PLATES (3)

10th c. AD
Silver. Gilded, engraved, stamped.
56 x 70mm.
Found in the city of Kiev, Vladimirskaya Street.
Excavated in 1901.
MHTU, inv. No. AZS 297-299.

Decorated with a lily pattern which for many ancient peoples was a symbol of nobility.

121. AQUAMANILE (Ewer)

1st half of 13th c. AD
Bronze. Cast, forged.
183 x 195mm.
Town of Chernigov.
Chance find.
From the collection of B.I. Khanenko.
NMHU, inv. No. v2001.

Used for religious purposes. This example is closely related to a number of northern German ewers of the 13th century.

122. AQUAMANILE (Ewer)

1st half of 13th c. AD
Bronze. Cast, forged.
240 x 200mm.
Town of Chernigov.
Chance find.
From the collection of B.I. Khanenko.
NMHU, inv. No. v2013.

In the shape of a centaur. The ewer was made in Lower Saxony.

123. CROSS

10th - 11th c. AD
Bronze. Cast, forged, engraved.
87 x 68mm.
Sivki Village, Chernigovski area, Chernigovskaya district.
Chance find.
NMHU, inv. No. v883.

Depicts the figure of Constantine.

123

124. CROSS

12th - 13th c. AD
Bronze. Cast.
110 x 65mm.
Date and location of find unknown.
NMHU, inv. No. v885.

The image is two-sided. On one side is a scene depicting the "Crucifixion of Christ". On the other side there is the figure of Mary with the infant Jesus. Such crosses were used to preserve the power of the saints, and were supposed to protect a person from evil.

125. BRACELET

11th - 13th c. AD
Silver. Forged, cast, soldered, nielloed, twisted.
Diameter - 80mm.
Kiev, Desyatinaya church.
Chance find, 1936.
MHTU, inv. No. SR-608.

126. TORQUE

11th - 13th c. AD
Silver. Forged, twisted, drawn wire.
Diameter - 160mm.
Chernishi village, Kanevski area, Cherkasskaya district.
Chance find, 1899.
MHTU, inv. No. SR-520.

127. TORQUE

11th - 13th c. AD
Silver. Forged, twisted, drawn wire.
Diameter - 185mm.
Date and location of find unknown.
MHTU, inv. No. SR-522.

135

128-133. "GRIVNI" (money ingots)

11th - 13th c. AD
Silver. Cast.
Length: AZS-2207-2208: 81mm; 75mm
AZS-2204-2205: 175mm; 165mm.
SR-502, 482: 128mm; 136mm.
Items AZS-2204, 2205, 2207, 2208: Kiev, Trekhsvetitelskaya Street.
Chance find, 1949.
Items SR-482, 502: Chubarov village, Chernigovskaya district.
MHTU, inv. No. AZS-2204, 2205, 2207, 2208; SR-482,502.

Ingots like these were in circulation until the beginning of the Mongol invasion.

134.   BREAST CHAIN

10th - 12th c. AD
Silver. Braided, cast, drawn wire.
Length - 680mm.
Found in Kiev.
Chance find.
MHTU, inv. No.SR-678.

135.   "KOLT" (head-dress pendant)

11th - 13th c. AD
Gold. Soldered, stamped, cloisonne' enamelled.
Diameter - 32 x 36mm.
Knyazha Gora settlement, Kanevski area, Cherkasskaya district.
Found in 1896.
MHTU, inv. No. DM-1773.

Contained perfume and thought to be imbued with protective powers.

140

136-137. "KOLTI" (head-dress pendants) (2)

138-139. "RYASNI" (Chains) (2)

11th - 13th c. AD
Gold. Soldered, stamped, cloisonne´ enamelled.
Kolti - diameter 45 x 31mm.
Ryasni - length 220mm.
Kolti: Knyazha Gora settlement, Kanevski area, Cherkasskaya district, 1897.
Ryasni: Sakhnovka village, Kanevski area, Kiev province, 1900.
MHTU, inv. No. DM-1838-1839, DM-1645-1646.

"Ryasni" and "kolti" were integral parts of royal head-dresses. Ryasni were fastened to the head-dress at the temple and reached to the shoulders. Kolti were suspended from their lower edges. (see illus. p. 63)

140.   "KOLT" (Head-dress pendant)

11th - 13th c. AD
Gold. Soldered, stamped, cloisonne´ enamelled.
Diameter - 49 x 58mm.
Kiev.
Chance find.
MHTU, inv. No. DM-7070.

Decorated with images of sacred birds, personifying kindness and prosperity.

141.   "KOLT" (head-dress pendant) in the shape of a star.

11th - 13th c. AD
Gold. Cast, forged, granulated, filigree.
Diameter - 43 x 36mm.
Chance find, Kiev, 1876.
From the collection of B.I. Khanenko.
MHTU, inv. No. DM-1774.

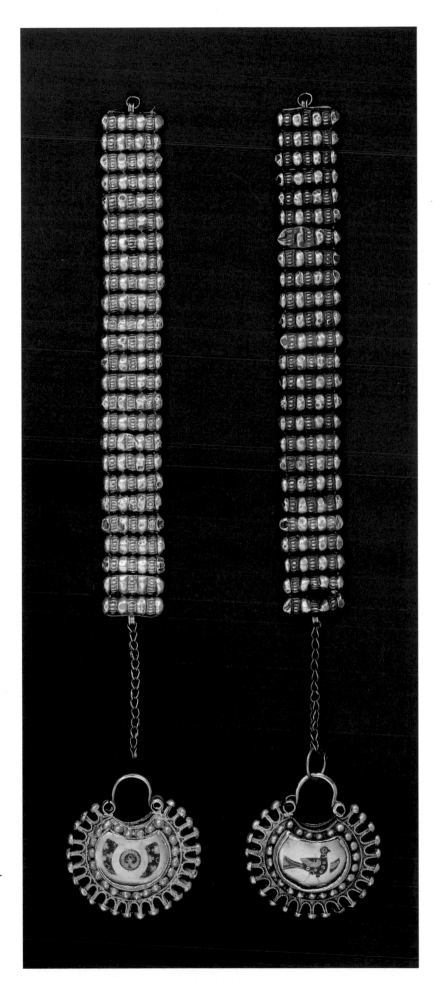

142-143. EAR PENDANTS

11th-13th c. AD
Gold. Granulated, filigree,drawn wire.
Diameter - 37.5 x 35mm; 36 x 35mm.
Khyazha Gora settlement, Kanevski area, Cherkasskaya district.
Chance find.
MHTU, inv. No. DM-6483-6484.

144.   EAR PENDANT

11th - 13th c. AD
Gold. Filigree, granulated, drawn wire.
38 x 40mm.
Found Knyazha Gora settlement, Kanevski area, Cherkasskaya district.
Chance find, 1897.
MHTU, inv. No. DM-1793.

145-146. EAR PENDANTS

11th - 13th c. AD
Gold. Filigree, granulated, drawn wire.
Diameter - 34mm (DM-6491); 41mm (AZS-406)
DM-6491 - Knyazha Gora settlement, Kanevski area, Cherkasskaya district.
AZS-406 - chance find.
MHTU, inv. No. DM-6491; AZS-406.

147.   EAR PENDANT

11th - 13th c. AD
Gold. Filigree, drawn wire, granulated, stamped.
47 x 44mm.
Kiev.
Chance find, 1938.
MHTU, inv. No. AZS-915.

148.   CHEST CHAIN AND PENDANT

12th - 13th c. AD
Gold. Stamped, drawn wire.
Length of chain - 420mm.
Pendant - 36 x 27mm.
Knyazha Gora, town of Kanev, Cherkasskaya district.
Chance find.
MHTU, inv. No. DM-1789; DM-6343.

Pendant in the form of a lily, a symbol of fertility.

151-152 (detail)

149.   TORQUE
12th - 13th c. AD
Gold. Forged.
185 x 190mm.
Sakhnovka village, Kornus-Shevchenkovski area, Cherkasskaya district.
Chance find, 1900.
From the collection of B.I. Khanenko.
MHTU, inv. No.DM-1636.

150.   TORQUE

12th - 13th c. AD
Gold. Forged.
215 x 220mm.
Sakhnovka village, Kornus-Shevchenkovski area, Cherkasskaya district.
Chance find, 1900.
From the collection of B.I. Khanenko.
MHTU, inv. No.DM-1637.

151-152. CHEST ICON WITH CHAIN

Cameo - Byzantium 12th c.AD
Mounting - Russian work from the 14th-15th century AD
Gold, silver, jet, garnet, quartz.
Carved, filigree.
Height of cameo with mounting - 66mm.
Length of chain - 680mm.
Date and location of find unknown.
From the collection of B.I. and V.N. Khanenko.
MHTU, inv. DM-1643, DM-1632.

Icon depicts the Mother of God, with the Greek inscription "Maiden Maria".

153

153. DRINKING CUP

12th c. AD
Byzantium (?)
Silver. Forged, embossed,
engraved, gilded, nielloed.
Height - 120 - 140mm
Diameter - 260mm.
Town of Chernigov.
Chance find, 1957.
MHTU, inv. No. AZS-1832.

*Richly decorated with mixture of
Byzantine and Eastern motifs.
Possibly buried at the time of the
Mongol invasion of Chernigov in
1239. The exact origin remains
unclear.*

141

154, 155

154. ARMBAND

Middle of 12th c. AD.
Silver. Forged, soldered, gilded,
engraved, nielloed.
Width - 45mm; diameter - 65mm.
Kiev, 10 Kudryavskaya street,
1986.
NMHU, inv. No. RDM-1556.

*Discovered in August 1986, the
hoard from which this and the
exhibits nos.155-161were taken,
consisted of 75 pieces. The motifs
reflect elements symbolic of both
pagan and Christian beliefs. One
of the masterpieces of applied art
of Kiev Rus.*

155. ARMBAND

Middle of 12th c. AD
Silver. Forged, granulated, sol-
dered, gilded.
Width - 45mm; diameter - 61mm.
Kiev, 10 Kudryavskaya street,
1986.
NMHU, inv. No. RDM-1557.

*The geometric designs of this arm-
band are unique in the applied art
of Kiev Rus.*

156. NECKLACE

Second half of 12th c. AD
Copper. Cast, gilded, cloisonne´
enamelled.
24 x 30mm.
Kiev, 10 Kudryavskaya street,
1986.
NMHU, inv. No. RDM-1576.

157. "KOLT". (head-dress pendant)

12th c. AD
Gold. Forged, cloisonne´ enamelled, soldered, stamped.
31 x 28mm.
Kiev, 10 Kudryavskaya street,
1986.
NMHU, inv. No. RDM-1579.

158. "RYASNA" (chain for pendant)

12th c. AD
Gold. Stamped, soldered.
Size of one" kolodochka" (cylinder
shaped link) - 11 x 6mm.
Kiev, 10 Kudryavskaya street,
1986.
NMHU, inv. No. RDM-1580.

159. NECKLACE

Second half of 12 c.AD
Gold. Forged, embossed, sol-
dered, filigree.
Size of beads: 17 - 25mm.
Kiev, 10 Kudryavskaya street,
1986.
NMHU, inv. No. RDM-1582-1604.

*As well as indicating a high posi-
tion in society, necklaces such as
these were regarded as amulets;
the circle symbolized eternity and
gold, perfection.*

160. DECORATIVE RING (Kiev type)

12th c. AD
Gold, pearls. Forged, granulated,
soldered, filigree.
28 x 30mm.
Kiev, 10 Kudryavskaya street,
1986.
NMHU, inv. No. RDM-1581.

*Belonged to a woman's ornamen-
tation, forming part of a ceremonial
costume. They were fastened to a
leather hoop or to a narrow band
with several rings in each strip.*

Ukrainian jewelry from the 16th to 18th centuries in the collection of the Museum of Historical Treasures of the Ukraine

The collection of gold and silver works of Ukrainian craftsmen of the 16th to early 20th centuries is one of the most interesting and comprehensive among all the remarkable jewelry preserved in the Museum of Historical Treasures of the Ukraine. It comprises a variety of secular and religious objects which are notable for the high level of workmanship and distinctive ornamentation.

The original collection comprised material in the Museum of Art and Antiquity, which became known in 1904 as the Kiev Museum of Arts, Industry and Science. After its reorganisation in 1924 it was renamed the Shevchenko All-Ukrainian Museum. After the revolution its collections were supplemented by gold and silver artefacts which were nationalised from private collections, museums, and the treasuries of Ukrainian monasteries and churches. Objects coming from those of the Pechersk Lavra and Cathedral of St Sophia in Kiev were of particular value from the artistic and historical point of view.

In 1969, in connection with the opening of the Museum of Historical Treasures of the Ukraine (a branch of the National History Museum of the Ukraine), the department of decorative applied arts of the 16th - 19th centuries received unique additions to its collection from the greatest museums of Kiev, Dnepropetrovsk, Simferopol, and many other cities.

This exhibition includes the work of goldsmiths and silversmiths of the 16th - 18th centuries which will acquaint the visitor with the centuries-long jewelry traditions of the Ukraine. The objects displayed demonstrate the distinctive national culture which developed from the artistic achievements of Kievan Rus.

Ukrainian jewelry developed in complex circumstances, when the nation had no state of its own and was occupied by neighbouring states - Lithuania, Poland, Hungary - and sustained attacks by Turkish and Mongol armies. The people's efforts to win freedom and independence, and to shake off the rule of foreign oppressors, took the form of the national liberation war of 1648-1654. In this struggle a powerful military force was augumented by Cossack units under the command of the hetman Bogdan Khmelnitskiy.

The national liberation movement was strongly supported by the Orthodox community which stood out against the Union of Orthodox and Catholic churches and religious oppression. It became the nucleus around which the progressive forces in the Ukrainian people united. Under its guidance the people's national self-consciousness developed, along with an acquaintance with humanism. In 1654 the war culminated in victory over Poland, and the Ukraine became united with Russia.

However, such a long-awaited peace did not bring tranquility to the Ukrainian lands. As a result of the Russo-Polish war of 1654-1667, Ukraine was once more partitioned. Ukraine east of the river Dnieper and Kiev remained part of the Russian state, while Ukraine west of the river became part of Poland. The Russian protectorate over the Left-bank Ukraine allowed it to preserve its autonomy (hetmanate) for a considerable time (from

1648 to 1764).

The development of Ukrainian jewelry in the 14th - 16th centuries occurred in complex historical circumstances. An important factor was the emergence of guilds among the craftsmen. In accordance with the Magdeburg Law, guilds for silversmiths and goldsmiths were founded in L'vov, Kiev, Chernigov, Lutska, Kamenets-Podolsk, and other towns. The rather few pieces of jewelry made during this period portray the influence of the West European styles, though given an original interpretation by local national traditions.

Jewelry from the 16th century reflects the transition from the Gothic style to the Renaissance. Craftsmen using such techniques as casting, engraving and gilding strove to fill the surface of objects with patterns composed of twining stems with short branches. Delicacy of execution distinguishes the graceful design on a seven-pointed throne cross from 1546. Such crosses were widely distributed in the Ukraine in the 16th - 17th centuries as a symbol of the maintenance of Orthodox belief (cat.no.161).

It should be noted that many works by Ukrainian craftsmen at this time reflected the pathos of the national liberation struggle. They treated in an especially penetrating and loving manner the scenes of Christian persecution and particularly the Crucifixion. In these scenes they conveyed with great understanding the drama of contemporary events and the depth of suffering of the principal actors.

In the second half of the 17th century secular art exercised a significant influence on the development of church plate. As a result, silversmiths began to show considerable interest in the real world and their surroundings. They abandoned a stylistic manner of portraying the saints. The former asceticism in their images disappeared and in their place appeared realistic details, individual facial features, and national costumes.

A feature of the art of this period was the changing nature of patronage. In addition to the hetmans, Cossack elders, and representatives of the Church, expensive pieces of jewelry were now being commissioned by ordinary Cossacks, the petty bourgeoisie, and village communities. This significantly furthered the rise of a culture coloured by popular tastes.

In accordance with the changing lifestyle of the hetmans and their circle, the range of silver and gold objects being made increased and became more varied. Such articles of regalia as pins and maces decorated with feathers, signifying senior rank among the Cossacks, were very popular among these purchasers. Gold buckles and studs became an integral part of ceremonial costume, and these had a great variety of shapes. For women in the aristocracy the craftsmen made gold crosses to be worn next to the skin, these being adorned with precious stones, and chains and necklaces decorated with enamelled images, and gold finger rings.

The Orthodox church was an important commissioner of ritual items. Many of the monastery treasuries in Ukrainian towns struck travellers by the abundance of their liturgical objects - crosses, chalices, patens, tabernacles, and decorated Gospel book covers. The way of life of the senior clergy was also notable for its opulence and luxury.

By the end of the 17th century there was a further strengthening of links between the leading Cossacks and the Orthodox church which played an important role in the spiritual life of society. The changing status of the new elite, which had become richer after the end of the 1648-1654 war, and their desire to be patrons, led to the renovation of old churches and the building of new stone ones, many of which were later to be recognised as outstanding pieces of architecture. The erection of new churches raised architecture to new heights, and it in its turn had a profound effect on painting, metal-working, wood-carving, and many other forms of the decorative applied arts.

Of great cultural importance for the Ukraine were the generous donations of money by the hetman Ivan Mazepa to various monasteries and churches. His activities as a patron encouraged numerous hetmans (Ivan Samoylovich, Danilo Apostol, Ivan Skoropadskiy), representatives of the civil and military elite (Radion Dumitrashko, Vasiliy Kochubey, Lizoguby) and many others to participate in church-building and also in their decoration. They commissioned gold and silver ritual objects of the highest artistic quality from both local craftsmen and those in other towns.

Fine proportions in the composition and rich execution are appealing features of the gold patens donated by the hetman Ivan Samoylovich to the Uspenskiy Cathedral of the Pechersk Lavra in Kiev. The technical perfection, harmony of the enamelled images, and insets of emeralds and rubies make this piece quite captivating (cat.no.165).

The jewelry of the 17th century which has come down to us indicates a wide acquaintance among the Ukrainian aristocracy with West European art. Many of the objects used for decorating silver icon frames, skladny (folding images of the saints), and crowns had been made in various jewelry-making centres in Europe and gifted to the church. A beautiful example of the jeweller's art is a gold pendant made by a German craftsman and bearing a representation of "The Miracle of St George". It was reworked by a Ukrainian craftsman and donated by the military leader Yakov Lizogub to a church in Chernigov. The image of St George is uncommonly expressive as he slays the winged dragon with a spear. The miniature figure is unusually lively and full of energy (cat.no.163).

Amongst the Ukrainian craftsmen gold open-work studs enjoyed great popularity. These were small metal rosettes with precious stones inset. Studs, and also semi-precious stones, including rubies, sapphires and emeralds, were imported into the Ukraine by Greek merchants. The craftsmen were fond of using the studs to decorate clothing. They were often fastened to the surface of gold objects, and in the 17th century were widely used on mitres. From the studs the jewellers assembled complicated ribbons decorated with stamped plant designs and enamelled images which gave the objects an unusual richness of colour. A good example of the use of studs is a 17th century silver mitre. In this piece the elegant decoration emphasizes its stately form (cat.no.164).

162

From the late 17th century the jewelry centre of the Ukraine was Kiev. Here worked such talented jewellers as Ivan Ravich, Yeremey Beletskiy, Ivan Atanazevich, Matvei Narunovich, and many others. The work of these craftsmen is distinguished by markedly individual styles, both succinct and expressive. Kievan workmanship exercised a strong influence on jewellers in other towns.

From the late 17th century Ukrainian art adopted the baroque style. Works of art from this period are marked by festivity, a superfluity of decoration, and original ornamentation in which there was a widespread introduction of local motifs - meticulously executed carnations, cornflowers and periwinkles, as well as raspberries, hips, and vines loaded with grapes. Some elements of the baroque style found fertile soil in the work of the well-known Kievan craftsman Ivan Ravich (1677-1762). A significant number of ritual pieces made by him for monasteries and churches have survived, as well as items for secular dignitaries. They are striking for their variety of form, sumptuous decoration, and interesting compositions.

A very high standard of workmanship is seen in a Gospel book cover decorated with saints. Ravich made good use of chiaroscuro in the stamped relief, and also through the colourful contrasts between the nielloed surface of the book cover and the gilded image itself (cat.no.169). A silver dish made by Ravich in 1723 displays fine workmanship and original ornamental motifs. The meticulously worked plant design successfully fills the surface around the central medallion which contains a representation of "The Miracle of the Archangel Michael" (cat.no.167).

The work of Ravich is distinguished by his special ability to harmonise the form of the object with its ornamentation. A vivid example of this is a silver chalice with an enamelled painted medallion. The relative proportions of the cup and base gives them a certain refinement. The expressive stamped ornament and the colourful range of enamelled medallions representing saints make this chalice exceptionally elegant (cat.no.168).

18th century jewelry was considerably influenced by book printing, engraving and architecture. Silversmiths willingly borrowed elements from book decoration and used images in their compositions from admired engravings. The appearance in Kiev of fine religious buildings served as sources of inspiration for silver tabernacles. Instead of treating these objects traditionally, making them in the form of a chest or a peasant hut, they modelled them on a far more magnificent structure - the bell tower. A tabernacle of 1756 is particularily original. It is striking in its strict proportions, enhanced by ornamentation and complex images. It is crowned by a pear-shaped cupola like that of the bell tower of the Pechersk Lavra Monastery in Kiev (cat.no.170).

During its development Ukrainian jewelry came into contact with the art of many Slav peoples. Close and friendly relations bound the Ukraine and Russia and encouraged the mutual enrichment of the two cultures. Magnificent examples of Russian silverwork found their way to the Ukraine, being given by tsars and civil and ecclesiastical feudal lords to the greatest monasteries and churches. Perfection in workmanship distinguishes a carved cross made from cypress and commissioned by the Russian tsar Fedor Alekseyevich in 1681. The delicate carving of the cypress wood and the ornate casing excites admiration of the craftsman's artistic ability(cat.no.166).

The flowering of the decorative applied arts in the Ukraine in the late 17th century led to the migration of Ukrainian craftsmen to Russian towns - silversmiths, wood-carvers, printers of books, and engravers. Under the influence of their creativity, there appeared in the decoration of Russian artefacts Ukrainian plant motifs - flowers of the field on succulent stalks, and spirally twisted or interwoven stems.

Ukrainian enamelwork also exerted an influence on that of Moscow. The artists of Moscow often copied Ukrainian examples of painted enamels, imitating the dark background and the bright colours of the Ukrainian pieces. Some of the more interesting examples of enamelwork are the medallions made by an unknown Kievan craftsman for ornamenting a silver chalice (cat.no.168). In creating enamelwork images on a religious theme, many jewellers found inspiration in the frescoes of churches.

The gold and silver works of art from the 16th-18th centuries included in the exhibition give a glimpse into one of the most interesting episodes in the development of Ukrainian jewelry. They also reflect the spirit and uniqueness of their talented creators.

161

162. PANAGIA

End of 17th c. AD, Ukraine
Gold, diamonds, sapphires,
rubies, corundums. Cast,
stamped, enamelled.
Length - 136mm; diameter -
64mm.
From the Sacristy of the
Chernigov diocese.
MHTU, inv. No. DM-5993.

*At the end of the 17th century
panagia (medallions) such as this
became even more ornamented
with the use of large numbers of
precious stones and brightly
coloured enamel. it would have
been worn on the chest by senior
members of the priesthood.
(Illus. p. 73)*

163. PENDANT/PANAGIA

17th c. AD, Germany, Ukraine
Gold, silver, emeralds, sapphires,
rubies, pearls. Cast, stamped,
enamelled.
Length - 115m; diameter - 85mm.
From the Sacristy of the Troitski
(Trinity) Monastery of the
Chernigov diocese.
MHTU, inv. No. DM-5990.

*The central image depicts St.
George slaying the dragon. Such
richly decorated pendants served
as accessories for men's and
women's ceremonial clothing. On
the inside, the owner's name is
inscribed - Yakov Lizogub, a
Chernigov colonel - who had the
pendant modified for church use.*

161. CROSS

1546, Ukraine
Silver, glass. Cast, engraved,
enamelled, gilded.
Height - 470mm; diameter -
235mm.
MHTU, inv. No. DM-6683.

*Intended for liturgical use. The
ornamentation shows a
Renaissance influence, and this
particular cross carries a craftsman's stamp, a feature which is
very rare for this period.*

163

164. MITRE

End of 17th c. AD, Ukraine
Silver, diamonds, emeralds,
rubies, sapphires, zircon, spinell,
turquoise, glass. Cast, stamped,
enamelled, gilded.
Height - 283mm; diameter of base
- 210mm.
MHTU, inv. No.DM-5969.

*Head-piece worn by the high
priesthood.*

165

164

76

165. PATEN

1686, Moscow.
Workshops of the Moscow Kremlin.
Gold, emeralds, rubies. Cast, stamped, engraved, enamelled.
Diameter - 230mm.
From the Sacristy of the Uspensk Cathedral of the Kievo-Pecherski Monastery.
MHTU, inv. No. DM-7866.

Dish for communion bread. One of the outstanding pieces from the workshops of the Moscow Kremlin. The central image depicts "The Lamb of God" in the form of the infant Jesus Christ, lying in a font, surrounded by angels, cherubs and the Holy Spirit in the shape of a dove.
Donated by Chief Ivan Samoyilovich in memory of his children. Damaged in 1941 during monastery evacuation because of aircraft bombing raids.

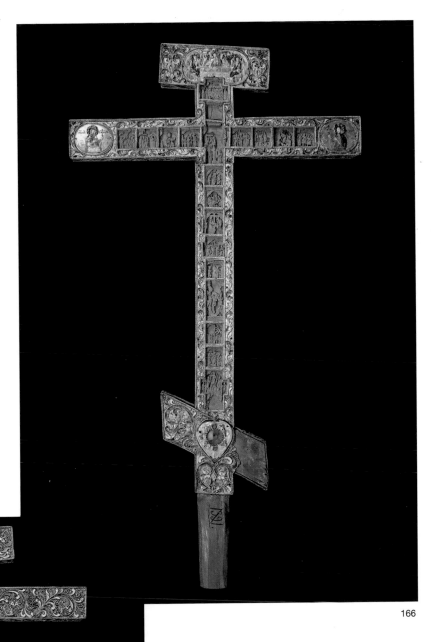

166

166. CROSS

1681, Moscow
Cypress, silver, glass. Embossed, gilded, filigree, carving on wood.
676 x 369 x 35mm.
Came from Dnepropetrovsk Historical Museum, 1967.
MHTU, inv. No. DM-7848-7852.

Decorated with 19 scenes from the life of Christ, carved in cypress wood. One of a group of rare works from the 17th century which are dated. Also inscribed is the name of the purchaser - the Russian Tsar Theodorus Alekseevich (born 1661).

167. PLATE

1723, Kiev
by Ivan Ravich.
Silver. Embossed, punched,
gilded.
Diameter - 440mm.
From the Sacristy of the
Vyidubetsk Monastery in Kiev.
MHTU, inv. No. DM-4599.

*Made on the orders of Father
Theodofilus Khomenko, Father
Superior of the Vyidubetsk
Monastery. The central medallion
depicts 'the Miracle of St. Michael'.
He is shown pushing a spear into
a rock crevice, from which flows a
stream of water.*

167

168

168. CHALICE

1830-1850, Kiev.
by Ivan Ravich.
Silver. Cast, embossed, punched,
enamelled, gilded.
Height - 345mm; diameter of base
- 170mm.
MHTU, inv. No. DM-340.

*The medallions on the cup depict
Christ, the Mother of God and
John the Baptist. On the base
they show images of Vasily Veliki,
Grigoriy Dvoeslova and Ioann
Zlatoyst.*

170

169.   GOSPEL BOOK COVER

First half of 18th c. AD, Kiev
by Ivan Ravich.
Paper, silver. Stamped, engraved,
nielloed, gilded.
450 x 290 x 60mm.
MHTU, inv. No.DM-448.

*Ornate Gospel book covers such
as this were made to be in harmony
with rich interior church fittings.
The central medallion depicts the
crucifixion scene, with images of
the Gospel writers in the four
corners.*

169

170.   TABERNACLE

1756, Kiev
Monogram of craftsman SS.
Silver. Cast, embossed, gilded.
165 x 125 x 240mm.
From the Sacristy of the Kievo-
Podolski church of Nikolai Dobri
(Nikolai the Kind).
MHTU, inv. No. DM- 4486.

*Intended for storing communion
bread. Designed to imitate
Ukrainian baroque architecture.
The side walls are decorated with
miniature scenes - 'Christ's entry
into Jerusalem', 'Placing into the
grave','the Last Supper', and 'the
washing of the disciples' feet'.*

171.   CROZIER

1730 - 1760, Kiev
by Matvei Narunovich.
Silver, glass, wood. Cast,
stamped, gilded.
Length - 915mm; diameter -
170mm.
MHTU, inv. No. DM-5.

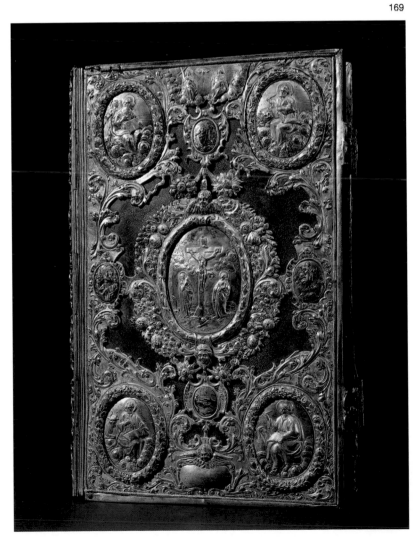